ROBERT SADLER
AND THE LOST
COPENHAGEN RUNNING GROUNDS
GARRATT LANE, WANDSWORTH

A story of early Pedestrianism and Athletics in South London

by

Kevin Kelly

DEDICATION
To Robin Sadler and his wife Margaret
Robin is the great, great, grandson of Robert Sadler
whose enterprise of 160 years ago led to the writing of this book.

Published by
Local History Publications
316 Green Lane
Streatham
London SW16 3AS
on behalf of Kevin Kelly
71 Penwortham Road
Streatham
London SW16 6RH

Text © Kevin Kelly 2013
Layout © Local History Publications 2013

ISBN 978 1 873520 93 2

CONTENTS

INTRODUCTION

Having lived in the borough of Wandsworth all my life and with a lifetime interest in both athletics and local history, I have for many years been intrigued by the athletics track which stood in or near Garratt Lane between 1853 and 1864 but whose considerable history had been lost with the passing of time.

It has been apparent for many years that although local historians were aware that a prominent athletics track, existed in Garratt Lane, nobody knew exactly where it had been located. A few years ago the Wandsworth library service even published a postcard for sale which was a reproduction of a Victorian poster advertising an event at the track. However, any enquiries at the local history studies library, the Wandsworth museum or the Wandsworth Historical Society made me realise that there was nobody who had found any concrete evidence of where the track had once stood.

My own theory was that it had either been in the Summerstown area or further up Garratt Lane towards Wandsworth town centre. For many years, although I had a number of clues, I had no clue by which I could absolutely, definitively identify where the track had once stood. The breakthrough came when I mentioned some of my clues to local historian David Ainsworth and he tied two of the clues together which led me into further research and an absolutely definitive identification of the site.

One of the clues I had given David was that I knew the owner of the track Robert Sadler operated from a building called *'The Wellington Inn'*. David then found evidence of the sale of Althorp Lodge in 1856 which clearly stated that the building for a while at least, was also called *'The Wellington Inn'*. Fortunately, although *'The Wellington Inn'* does not appear on any known maps, Althorp Lodge appears on numerous ones, so the mystery was solved once I knew that this building had for a time held this dual name.

My research then led me into countless hours spent at Battersea Local History Studies Library, The London Metropolitan Archives, Colindale National Newspaper Library, Westminster Reference Library, numerous cemeteries and their archives, and books written by 'local history' and 'athletics' historians. It was a fascinating journey to discover so much about the history of the Sadler family, the scope of well over 500 events held at the venue during its eleven years existence, the exciting but sometimes murky world of Victorian professional athletics and the very interesting history of the Summerstown area.

So many people have been helpful in a variety of ways and I would particularly like to mention and thank prominent athletics historians:- Peter Lovesey, Warren Roe, Dave Terry and Alex Wilson. Local historians:- David Ainsworth, Janis Benson, Paul Dong, Tony Fletcher, Graham Gower and Tony Shaw. Also, the Rev Dr Roger Ryan Vicar of St Mary's Church, Summerstown and various staff at Wandsworth Heritage Service, The British Library Colindale, Evershed Funeral Directors, Islington Local History Library, Lambeth Cemetery Blackshaw Road, London Metropolitan Archives, Perrott Grenville Ltd., formerly at 811 Garratt Lane, Putney Vale Cemetery, The Probate Registry, Westminster Archives Centre and the Westminster Reference Library.

Marion Gower was particularly helpful to me with genealogical research as I strived to find and contact Robert Sadler's descendents. The breakthrough on this front came when Marion gave me a contact number for Robin Sadler a great, great, grandson of Robert and now living on the Isle of Man. He was very interested in my project and most generous with his time when I visited him and his wife Margaret. A wonderful painting he owned of Robert 'Bob' Sadler, was the first illustration I had ever seen of a member of the Sadler family that I had spent so many years researching.

Despite Althorp Lodge having stood in Garratt Lane for over 100 years, I have been unable to find a drawing, painting or photograph of it, so I am immensely grateful to another local historian Colin Fenn, who armed with what information I had available and with his considerable artistic expertise was able to provide me with a representation of how Althorp Lodge and the attached ground would have looked in its heyday as a sporting facility. I am also grateful for the artistic ability of Fay Whiting who coloured the race illustration which has helped bring the cover of this book to life.

The whole project has only reached closure with the immense help given to me by the outstanding local historian 'Mr Streatham' John W Brown, whose local knowledge of South London, his skill and expert guidance in publishing and his patient attention to detail has finally brought the project to fruition.

I sincerely hope that this book will appeal to those with an interest in both early athletics and local history and that it will fill a gap of knowledge that was previously lacking in the annals of Wandsworth's proud history.

Kevin Kelly

Portrait and signature of Robert Sadler (c1813-1896)
(Courtesy of Robin Sadler).

CHAPTER 1

Nineteenth century communication and the sport of Pedestrianism

In early nineteenth century England posting letters was not an easy matter. In the London Directory of 1826 it records that letters had to be taken to 'The Two Penny Post Receiving Houses' for districts in London and suburbs whereas letters for the country had to be taken to 'General Post Receiving Houses'. Rates on country letters varied according to distance. adhesive stamps were not introduced until 1841 and prior to that, anyone sending letters was advised to see them stamped before leaving the Receiving Office. Persons posting bank notes were advised to cut them in half and not post the second half until receipt of the first half had been acknowledged.

Pigot's directory of 1838 showed two receiving houses in Wandsworth, *'Mary Foster's'* in the High Street and *'The French Horn & Half Moon'* in East Hill both received four deliveries a day except Sunday from London and had two dispatches morning and afternoon each day except Sunday.

In Lower Tooting, the receiving house was *'Thomas Watkinson's'* in the High Street who received three deliveries a day except Sunday and had two dispatches as in Wandsworth.

Apart from the mail, the best way to distribute information was either through posters, handbills or newspapers.

1) The offices of the sporting newspaper *'BELL'S LIFE IN LONDON'* in the Strand.

For sporting events in particular this meant newspapers such as *'Bell's Life in London'*, *'The Illustrated Sporting News'* and *'The Era'*.

Inns and Taverns were often used as starting points for Mail and Stage coaches on their long journeys to all parts of England, Wales and Scotland and were also commonly used as centres of sporting activity. Pigot's Directory in 1838 showed Wandsworth was served by daily stage coaches at regular intervals to and from central London. *'The Spread Eagle'*, *'The Ram'* and *'The Kings Head'* in Wandsworth town and *'The Angel'* at Lower Tooting were the local departing and arrival points.

Mr Shillibeer's bus service in central London didn't begin until 1829 and it was many years before the London suburbs received any form of public road transport. The telegraph system was continuing to

develop and was certainly used by newspapers to transmit news and even carrier pigeons would have been used for the same purpose.

For centuries men had competed against each other in various athletic contests at rural sports and the 'Athletics' or 'Track & Field' that we know today had its foundations in these pastimes. By the eighteenth century, it became commonplace for men to challenge each other to all manner of contests either to beat each other or to achieve performances that would be considered difficult. Sometimes, instead of man to man racing there would be contests of a man pitting himself only against the watch, backing himself to achieve a certain task within a specified time. The challenges and the responses appeared regularly in the sporting papers which was the quickest way to transmit any information. Wagers would be made and betting on the result would be rife. Because of this gambling aspect, huge crowds would be attracted to these events and these early athletes, whether runners or walkers, became known to the public as 'Pedestrians'. Unlike a modern athletics meeting with a range of events to view, at many of these early contests there might only be one race to watch but still the crowds would pour in through the gates and vast sums would be laid in bets on the outcome. The sport of Pedestrianism was not seasonal and events were arranged throughout the whole year quite regardless of weather conditions.

Quite often the wagers would be made between men for whom it was not their main source of income and would merely be the way of settling an argument or a boast. Many others did consider it their profession and for some their ability was to enable them to become very wealthy men. Their fame led to some of them adopting, or being given, fancy names which were usually attached to their profession or place of residence. *'The Regent Street Pet'*, *'Young England'*, *'The Norwich Milkboy'*, *'The Billingsgate Boy'* and *'The American Deer'* were some of this group who were only occasionally advertised by their proper names of John Smith, Teddy Mills, John Brighton Sam Barker and William Jackson and all of whom competed at Robert Sadler's track in Garratt Lane.

2) The well known pugilist Tom Spring's *'Castle Tavern'* in Holborn was one of the sporting houses where the public and various sporting men could meet to discuss the latest news, make wagers and meet the sporting personalities of the day. It was quite common for sportsmen to become publicans either during or after their heyday. This drawing of Tom Spring's Parlour also clearly depicts how the latest sporting prints could be shown off and where copies could be purchased.

Articles for these challenge races would be drawn up and on their mutual agreement would be signed by the competitors. The articles would stipulate the various terms agreed to such as venue, start time, method of start, and of course the amount of the wager. Stakes from the contestants would usually be held by publicans at the sporting houses or by the editors of the established sporting newspapers. These stakes would usually be paid to the stakeholders in instalments and the sporting press would inform their readership of the progress of these arrangements. The phrase 'a side' followed the amount that was been wagered by either side of the bet and this information would also be publicised.

It was not possible to reproduce photographs in newspapers until the late 1880's but it was possible to print line drawings. Therefore, many talented artists would be employed to make accurate line drawings from existing photographs which could then be printed. Pedestrians and other sportsmen were regular visitors to *'Bell's Life'* in the Strand and very close by in Newcastle Street were the photographic studios of George Newbould. Here, and of course at other photographic studies, the famous sportsmen would sit for their portraits. Cabinet cards and smaller cartes de visites could be sold to the public and the skilled artists would reproduce them as line drawings for publication in the sporting press. These drawings, often produced as supplements or inserts, were in themselves collectable and lent themselves to enhancement by colour tinting and framing.

**3) TOM SPRING
1795-1851**

In his memoirs written in 1899, Robert Watson, a former editor of *'The Sporting Life'*, recalls the time when Sam Barker *'The Billingsgate Boy'* and another well known pedestrian Harry Andrews, had arranged to meet at *'Bell's Life'* with the intention of making a match to race each other. The nerves of each man were affected by this meeting and while the nerves caused Barker to shake his head, they caused Andrews to wink. Whenever Sam made a proposition it caused Andrews to significantly blink both eyes and directly Andrews proffered a suggestion, Barker shook his head. There was some difficulty in coming to a mutual understanding of the terms and what with the winking on the part of Andrews and the head shaking on the part of Barker, the chairman, believed to be Vincent Dowling, came to the conclusion that the men were not treating him as a gentleman and in consequence, ordered them to leave the room.

The most popular day for these sporting events to be held was a Monday but with the agreement of everyone concerned, matches were arranged on any suitable day of the week. Starting times were agreed and publicised but on numerous occasions contestants would appear well after the starting time which had been announced. The crowds would be prepared to wait for their appearance as it was unlikely that they would not appear at all and forfeit their stake money. The betting aspect and the consumption of alcohol could turn these gatherings into very rowdy affairs and the sport of Pedestrianism did not have a good name amongst the general public who considered it a lower class sport. With money at stake, the sport was open to corruption by unscrupulous pedestrians, backers and followers alike. If there was any suspicion of malpractice, letters would flood into the sporting press and efforts would be made to curtail the activities of certain individuals.

Public Houses played a huge part in sporting life, acting as a meeting place for followers of sport and were often managed by promoters, athletes or ex

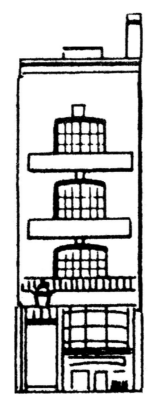

4) Thomas Wilson's public house *'The Spotted Dog'* at 298 in the Strand, the main public house in London for the promotion of Pedestrianism.

5) THOMAS WILSON (1814-1866)

athletes. Thomas Wilson was the proprietor of *'The Spotted Dog'* in the Strand which was the most famous Pedestrian public house in London along with *'The Proud Peacock'* managed by Jesse Smith adjoining the Adelphi Theatre by Bull Inn Court in Maiden Lane off Southampton Street in Covent Garden. These proprietors would often act as stakeholders for the contestants and frequently act as referees for the contests. The pedestrians themselves would frequent the pubs and often display their trophies there.

Officials for the contests were sometimes selected only just prior to the start of events by searching amongst those present and who had to be agreed by both parties. Quite often the owner of the facility would be appointed as the neutral referee and he would be there to see that all the articles of agreement were adhered to and his decisions would be the ultimate arbitrator in the event of a close finish or of any other dispute. Often he was positioned in a structure built so that he would have an elevated view of the course and particularly of the finish line. His decisions, would of course decide the various wagers laid by the pedestrians and the public and his neutrality would be crucial. On numerous occasions his decisions would lead to heated arguments and quite often he would be physically threatened. In the event of a match made for a pedestrian to race against 'time', a timekeeper would obviously be required but apart from these matches, the watch was not often in evidence and many races were never timed at all as the main purpose of the events were merely to decide a winner and the speed at which they ran or walked was considered of no consequence. The top athletes however were quite often timed and this led to the setting up of records for the most popular distances.

The costume in which these men competed gradually became standardised and took the form of a long sleeved vest (guernsey), long leggings with briefs over the top and rubber soled or spiked shoes. Sometimes the pedestrians chose to run bare-chested but would not do so if ladies were to be present. Running tracks at the time were not of a standardised distance and varied in quality and indeed shape. Grass was the usual surface but eventually dirt or cinder tracks became the norm.

Two men sprint races were often started by the mutual consent of the competitors and this often led to long delays as the combatants feinted and dodged about seeking to gain an advantage. Because of this, gun starts gradually became routine and starting methods such as 'the drop of a handkerchief' and 'the drop of a hat' faded into history.

Many of these contests would take place on the public roads until this was banned in 1850. The ban led to the introduction of events in confined areas such as commons or on enclosed grounds where a sturdy fence would allow the owner or promoter to charge an entry fee. So it was that the running tracks we are familiar with today were born. Until the 1860's the sport was virtually all professional but amateurs, in particular from the Oxford and Cambridge colleges were beginning to organise sports of their own.

In 1864 the first Oxford University v Cambridge University athletics match took place on a strictly amateur basis and the Universities and Public Schools pushed for the formation of a governing body which was eventually achieved in 1880 with the foundation of the AAA (Amateur Athletic Association) who would set about formulating rules and regulations to govern the sport with the strict provision that no athletes would compete for money and that no betting should take place on the ground. The professional sport

6) Site of 'The Proud Peacock' the public house in Maiden Lane by the side of Bull Inn Court which still leads through into the Strand next to the Adelphi Theatre.

struggled on but had become more and more disreputable and finally ended, at least in the south of England, with the riot and destruction of the Lillie Bridge ground in Seagrave Road, West Brompton in 1887 when the sprinters Hutchens and Gent had failed to appear for an advertised match. The crowd rioted, setting fire to the buildings which comprised the stadium and no event was ever held there again. The area is now a car park to cater in particular as an overflow car park for Earls Court.

Prior to 1880, numerous tracks in London had catered for the professional sport and a very well known one existed within easy reach of Wandsworth town centre. It was only to last eleven years from 1853 until 1864 but during that period, many of the most famous pedestrians of the day competed there. In the final years of its life it was known as 'The Copenhagen Grounds, Garratt Lane' and the founder of this sporting facility was a local man Robert Sadler but more of him later.

7) JESSE SMITH, proprietor of 'The Proud Peacock' in Maiden Lane.

CHAPTER 2
Smithfield Market
and the Copenhagen House Running Grounds Islington

By the middle of the nineteenth century London's main market for the sale of animal livestock and which had stood in the city for over 800 years had become a very dangerous and unhealthy place. Live cattle, pigs, horses and sheep being herded through the busy London streets were often responsible for injuries and deaths. Slaughter houses on site meant that blood and refuse ran down the narrow streets towards the open Fleet Ditch where Farrington Road now stands and was causing an obvious health hazard.

The ever growing population of London had increased the demand for meat and by the 1840's the extension of the railway system and the use of steam boats meant that travel into central London in some cases was reduced from ten days for drovers on the road, to just twelve hours in relative comfort on a train or boat.

The danger, smell and noise had become unbearable especially for residents of Smithfield. Some of the dealing was being done in local streets as the market which only covered six acres, was far too small to contain all the animals. Something had to be done and a new site had to be found to resolve the problem. An attempt had been made to solve this by John Perkins of Bletchingley, who had opened the Islington Cattle Market on a fifteen acre site in 1836 but his venture had failed and after a few years in operation it had closed. It would take nearly another twenty years before the Smithfield market problem would eventually be resolved.

In eighteenth century London the Copenhagen Fields in Islington were a popular venue for large public meetings. In the centre of the space was Copenhagen House so named, it is though, following the visit of the King of Denmark to the court of James 1 in 1606 when the house was built as accommodation for Danish visitors. By the mid eighteenth century, the area also accommodated pleasure grounds and tea gardens. In addition it was also popular for Sports such as Cricket, Skittles, Fives, Dog-fighting, Bear-baiting and various Highland Games.

The cricket ground had been opened in 1835 and by 1841 an enclosed Shooting Ground had been added. By late May 1849 John Garratt, a Staffordshire man, became the owner and in March 1850 he announced reduced prices for cricket and other sports. He built a 200 yard sprint track which he opened in September 1850 and during the next winter he laid out a gravel track measuring one third of a mile around the cricket ground and also built an eight foot fence to surround it so as to be able to charge admission. He was able to open this track on March 17 1851 and for the next two years it became the main pedestrian track in London and was commonly known as *'The Old Cope'*.

John Garratt's innovation of organising races for Championship Belts was a huge success. On March 22 1852 16,000 people paid to watch a 10 miles championship race between George Frost and John Levett with possibly a further 9,000 watching from vantage points outside. On July 26 in the same year, Charles Westhall became the world's first sub 4:30 miler with a time of 4:28. It would take nearly another 102 years before Roger Bannister would break the magic four minutes.

To solve the Smithfield Market livestock problem it had been decided that the Copenhagen Fields in Islington would provide the solution with the construction of a new market there to leave Smithfield to remain just as a meat market. In December 1852 a severe storm did enormous damage at the grounds and they finally closed on March 21 1853. Work was soon begun on the New Metropolitan Cattle Market but during its brief life, the Copenhagen Athletic Ground had seen all records from one to ten miles beaten.

8) A drover driving his sheep and cattle through the streets of London to Smithfield Market.

9) A race at John Garratt's Copenhagen ground in Islington.

10) The last day at SMITHFIELD MARKET.

On Monday June 11 1855 the last livestock market was held at Smithfield and the New Metropolitan Cattle Market, having been constructed by the City of London Corporation at a cost of £300,000, was opened by Prince Albert. It was a thirty acre site and had been chosen for its proximity to the goods yard of the newly opened Great North Eastern Railway and North London Railway to the north of Kings Cross, where livestock could easily be transported by train and then driven the short distance that remained from the rail depots to the market. On market days in excess of 15,000 animals could be traded. It would later to be known as Caledonian Market.

There was 13,000 feet of railing to which about 6,000 beasts could be tied comfortably and 1.800 pens which could hold up to 35,000 sheep, a considerable extent of sheds for lairage and two spacious slaughter houses as well as a complete system of drainage and sewerage and an ample supply of fresh water.

'The Illustrated London News' of June 16 1855 wrote:

'It was indeed high time that something like system was introduced into the livestock market of London, where packing sheep into haylofts, slaughtering them in cellars, filling sewers with garbage, driving mad bullocks down the Old Bailey and blocking up the Barbican with foot-sore worn out beasts had become an intolerable nuisance'.

The *'Old Cope'* athletic ground in Islington was now history but the Smithfield Market problem had been solved.

11) THE METROPOLITAN CATTLE MARKET Islington, built on the site of the Copenhagen Fields to overcome the problems at Smithfield Market.

CHAPTER 3
Summerstown and the Sadler family of Wandsworth

In the late eighteenth century the South London village of Wandsworth was still a quaint and old fashioned place. It was also however the centre of several important industries, many introduced there by the Huguenot refugees who had come into the district to escape religious persecution in France. They were attracted to the Wandsworth area by the fast flowing river Wandle and its mills. In fact, it was considered the busiest river for its size in Europe and was renowned for the special quality of its water so important in dyeing and bleaching and also for its good flow to drive the water wheels, hardly ever drying up in the summer, or freezing in the winter. There were industries of calico printing, hat making, oil mills, paper works, dye works, corn mills, brewing and vinegar making amongst others. Despite all this industry, late eighteenth and early nineteenth century Wandsworth still consisted mainly of farmland, market gardens, grand estates and the open heaths of Wandsworth and Wimbledon commons.

In the early years of the nineteenth century Garratt Lane, originally known as South Street, was the road which led in a southerly direction out from Wandsworth village centre to the even smaller village of Tooting and on its journey passing through the small hamlets of Dunsford, Garratt and Summerstown. An ancient tithe map shows the spelling of the name of this small community as 'Somers Town' but this became 'Summers Town' or 'Summerstown' so spelt, it is believed, to distinguish it from the 'Somers Town' in North London. Another theory is that because the Wandle was so prone to frequent flooding in the winter that the summer months were the only time that the area was habitable. It was not a wealthy area and consisted of small, mostly wooden cottages, with hard working but basically poor residents numbering some 750 many of whom were employed in the various industries which were very dependent on the nearby river, the hamlet of Summerstown and its residents were known in particular for their participation in the silk printing industry.

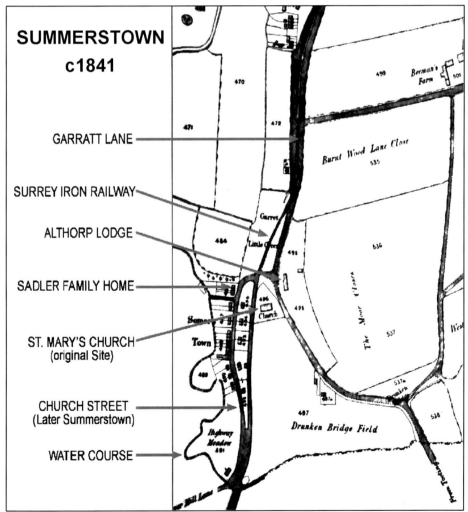

Before 1835, the community in this area had neither a church nor a school and were therefore were without any means of education, the nearest church and school would have involved the rather long trek into central Wandsworth which was nearly two miles away, or the rather shorter journey to Tooting. In fact, the Summerstown area was sometimes described as Lower Tooting and was right on the edge of the boundary with the Streatham parish.

For the community, a local church and school were badly needed and thanks to the generosity of a local man, Joshua Stanger, this was achieved in 1835 when he provided all the funds necessary for the erection of a building which would serve as a school room during the week but which could be used as a chapel on a Sunday according to the rites of the Church of England.

SUMMERSTOWN c1841

GARRATT LANE

SURREY IRON RAILWAY

ALTHORP LODGE

SADLER FAMILY HOME

ST. MARY'S CHURCH (original Site)

CHURCH STREET (Later Summerstown)

WATER COURSE

12) Tithe map of c1841, showing the sparse neighbourhood of Summerstown. (Courtesy of Wandsworth Heritage Service).

This church and sometime school was built in the Lancet style of architecture with a square tower surmounted by a small octagonal spire at the west end and it occupied a prominent site at the junction of Garratt Lane and the road now called Summerstown but then known as Church Street. In 1838 he added a Vicarage (Parsonage) and in 1841 a Day School which meant that the original dual purpose building then became solely a 220 seat church which in 1845 was consecrated by the Lord Bishop of Winchester as the Parish Church of St Mary's, Summerstown. After the ceremony the Bishop, clergy and the numerous gentry present, sat down to a slap up dinner in the Day School.

In addition, Mr Stanger also had a house built for the master and mistress of the school and provided an endowment of £200, the interest of which could be used as a fund for church repairs and insurance. Later, when larger schools had been built in Wandsworth, the old school became redundant and both the school and the headmaster's house were purchased by the church for use as a Church Hall and a Sunday School. Following a long drought in 1893 which caused serious damage to buildings throughout London, the old church was found to have very weak foundations and was condemned by the London County Council. Many members of the congregation opposed a demolition, instead preferring to spend money in under pinning the old building rather than constructing a new church but despite their opposition and as it was the cheaper of the two options, a decision was taken to demolish it and build a new place of worship. The congregation then used a

13) ST MARY'S CHURCH Summerstown built in 1835 which stood at the junction of Church Street (later Summerstown) and Garratt Lane. Following the very dry summer of 1893 it was deemed to be a dangerous structure and was demolished. (Courtesy of Wandsworth Heritage Service).

temporary 'Iron Church' which was erected behind the school until 1899 and subsequently used the Church Hall, before the present St Mary's Church on a completely new site at the corner of Wimbledon Road and Keble Street was constructed and eventually opened in 1904. Many items from the old church including the Font, were incorporated into the new building and can still be seen there today.

For many years, other than the cottages in Church Street which backed on to the site, the old church, the parsonage and the school were the only structures on the triangle of land fronting on to Garratt Lane between where the Prince of Wales Public House stood and the St Clement Danes Almshouses now stand.

Until its closure in 1846, the tracks of the Surrey Iron Railway ran between the cottages on the east side of Church Street and these three buildings. It was not a passenger railway but constructed at a cost of £24,000 to enable coal and other goods to be transported from Wandsworth out to Croydon and Merstham while country produce could be brought back to Wandsworth on the return journey. The railway, acknowledged by some as the first public railway in the world, had opened in 1803 and was considered to be the wonder of its time with up to five wagons being pulled on tracks by a single horse. Towards the end of the nineteenth century and into the early years of the twentieth century, there was an explosion of building and the laying out of Keble Street in 1902 virtually bisected this triangle as dozens of new houses were built as well as the new St Mary's Church.

14) An Illustrated London News drawing of the ST CLEMENT DANES ALMSHOUSES when they were first erected in 1849 which clearly shows the rural nature of Garratt Lane at the time.

The vicars of St Mary's Summerstown parish in those Victorian times were:- 1835 Edward Whitley, 1848 Richard Chambers, 1859 Charles Harris, 1872 George Stanham, 1876 Lewis Morgan 1887 John Morton and 1899 John Robinson. The various Baptisms, Weddings and Funerals presided over by these clergy, would have made them very familiar with many members of a prominent local family who had a long association with the area both as residents and business men, this family carried the surname of Sadler.

Born in 1786 to William and Elizabeth Sadler, James Sadler was a Wandsworth man and was employed as a calico printer. His wife Ann hailed from Great Yarmouth and she was the eldest of four children born to Robert Rook Spinney and Ann Harman. The tithe map and the census of 1841, show that James Sadler lived with his family in Church Street in the village of Somers Town, the small cottage where they lived still stands as number six at the northern end of the winding little road we now call Summerstown. Numbers six and eight are the oldest buildings left in the road while 'The Corner Pin' public house next to them was built in 1924 and replaced a much earlier beer house that stood on this site during the time the Sadler family were in number six. It stands on the corner of Riverside Road, a lane that in the 1850's led down to the Garratt Print works where many of the Church Street residents would have been employed. A small stream with its origins in the Springfield area, crossed Garratt Lane at the marvellously named Drunken Bridge, meandered along what is now Wimbledon Road and then ran behind the cottages further down Church Street before crossing Riverside Road and finding its way into the river Wandle. The two willow trees now standing at the entrance to the Greyhound Stadium complex at the beginning of

Plough Lane perhaps betray the existence of this water course which now runs in a culvert underground and which prior to the construction of the Greyhound Stadium, fed the watercress beds that covered the area behind the gardens of the cottages on the west side of Church Street.

For the 1841 census, this tiny cottage housed James and Ann, their three sons James, Robert and William and two of their three daughters Elizabeth and Rachel, the third daughter Ann appears to have died at a very young age. Also living there were Robert's wife Jane and their one year old baby son John and Ann's younger sister Rachel Rook Spinney. The youngest of the Sadler family Rachel, was to move away and was living in Lower Marsh, Lambeth at the time of her marriage to a butcher Joseph Banister in 1848.

Running virtually parallel with Garratt Lane was the river Wandle which drove the various mills strung along its length and the local industries of bleaching, printing and dyeing of calicos were well supplied with men from the small communities of Garratt and Summerstown. Like their father, who was a silk printer, the three sons of James were also employed in the printing trade, the eldest James was a silk and woollen printer, Robert was a dyer and William like his father was also a calico printer.

The middle son Robert was particularly interested in sport and was known locally as a useful pugilist and pedestrian. In March 1839 he had married Jane Hughes at All Saints Church in Fulham and prior to their marriage they had a baby daughter Ellen, born in August 1838, who had only survived for six weeks. They had come to live with his parents at Church Street in Somers Town with their son John born in 1840. Before the end of the 1840's Robert's career

15) A 1924 plan for the rebuilding of 'The Corner Pin' in Summerstown but showing the footprint of the previous building and the two cottages.

16) The pair of cottages at the northern end of Summerstown next to 'The Corner Pin' public house. The Sadler family were living in the right hand one (now number 6) at the time of the 1841 census.

had changed direction and he had moved further down Church Street where, on the other side of the road, he was managing 'The Sir Jeffrey Dunstan', a beer house owned by Young and Bainbridge at number 22. The Young and Bainbridge partnership lasted from 1831 until it was dissolved in 1884 after which the brewery traded only under the name of Young's and their numerous public houses became a prominent feature of the Wandsworth landscape.

Just after the demise of the Surrey Iron Railway, four groups of three cottages each, had been built between the spaces of the four pairs of existing cottages on the eastern side of Church Street which had backed on to the railway track and on Thursday October 24 of 1850 this continuous line of twenty cottages came up for sale at an auction held at 'The Spread Eagle' Wandsworth. The sale notice notified prospective purchasers that particulars of the properties could be found at various places including from Robert Sadler at 'The Sir Jeffrey Dunstan' who would also be able to show people around the properties. There was an artesian well situated in front of 'The Sir Jeffrey Dunstan' and all the cottage residents, who obviously had no running water themselves, had free access to this well. Robert himself purchased the two cottages next to his beer house for £190. These were numbers 20 and 21 and his parents James and Ann, his brother James and his sister Elizabeth came to live in number 21. The 1851 census shows Robert living at 'The Sir Jeffrey Dunstan', with his wife Jane and their two children John (11) and Martha (7).

In 1887, Church Street was renumbered and its name was changed to 'Summerstown'. As a consequence numbers 21 and 22 became numbers 45 and 47.

It is worth recording that the premises run by Robert known as 'The Sir Jeffrey Dunstan' was so called in memory of a man who had become a local legend and was the penultimate 'Mayor' of Garratt. Despite being a local man, Robert or his parents would never have seen 'Sir' Jeffrey Dunstan as his two time election as

'Mayor' had been in 1781 and 1785. He had been a very popular spoof Mayor in the eighteenth century fun and games that surrounded the mock elections on Garratt Green which attracted up to 100,000 people to the area with their coaches, carts and horses clogging up all the roads leading to the green where the 'Mayor' would be crowned. Jeffrey was described as 'a grotesque dwarf about four feet tall with a large head' and by profession was a second-hand wig seller. However, he was reputed to have had a devilish wit and an ability to give amusing speeches. His eventual demise, when he suffocated while intoxicated and being pushed in a wheelbarrow, was a strange and peculiar end. The tales of the various exploits of 'Sir Jeffrey' were obviously enshrined in local folklore.

17) A caricature of SIR JEFFREY DUNSTAN elected the spoof Mayor of Garratt at the end of the 18th century. (Courtesy of Wandsworth Heritage Service).

In 1852, less than two hundred yards away from 'The Sir Jeffrey Dunstan' at the Garratt Lane end of Church Street was the newly built public house 'The Prince of Wales' covering land where previously had been the railway track of the Surrey Iron Railway. On the opposite and eastern side of Church Street lying back from the road and facing Garratt Lane, was the church of St Mary's Summerstown while on the other side of Garratt Lane directly opposite 'The Prince of Wales" stood a large building known as Althorp Lodge.

The exact origins of Althorp Lodge are lost in antiquity but it was certainly constructed before the end of the eighteenth century and might have initially been a farmhouse. The Spencer family were Lords of the manor and the house was probably named after their family seat in Northamptonshire although the family themselves appear to have had no direct connection with it. The land it stood on was owned by Deeble Dutton and by the 1830's the building was rented to Mr Thomas Lewis, was being used as a school and known locally as 'Mr Lewis's Academy'. By 1851, a provision merchant, Edward Stuart had taken up residence but within a couple of years Althorp Lodge had become the home of Robert Sadler and his family.

18) 'THE SIR JEFFREY DUNSTAN' public house at 47 Summerstown during its later life after it had served its time as a public house. During Bob Sadler's tenure of the property the address would have been 22 Church Street. (Courtesy of Wandsworth Heritage Service).

CHAPTER 4
The New Surrey Pedestrian Grounds and the Wellington Inn Garratt Lane

It was very common for sports facilities to be situated near public houses where the publicans would gain, not only from the admission prices to an enclosed ground but also from the alcohol sales at their premises. Robert Sadler, as the new tenant of Althorp Lodge, decided to give it the alternative name of *'The Wellington Inn'* and to operate the building as a beer house and he moved into the premises with his wife and two children. His son John was working as a keeper at the Surrey Lunatic Asylum, later to become Springfield Hospital, but John was subsequently to change his profession and like his father become a beer retailer, while Robert's daughter Martha would work as a barmaid at *'The Wellington'*.

Robert Sadler's interest in sport and Pedestrianism in particular, gave him the idea of establishing a pedestrian facility locally and he found land available for the purpose in the field behind Althorp Lodge facing Garratt Green and known as *'The Moor Close'* which, like Althorp Lodge, was also owned by Deeble Dutton.

The Beer Act of 1830 had been brought in to stimulate growth in a time of national economic decline. Successive governments had always levied tax on the sale and production of alcohol but it was now decided to relax some of these restrictive trade laws. Any rate payer could now set up a beer house provided that they paid the licence fee. It was hoped that this would make beer cheaper, undermine the market for smuggled wine and spirits, encourage people to drink beer instead of gin and bring in extra revenue through the licence fee. This caused an explosion in the number of beer houses and many were set up in private houses quite often using nothing more than a front or back room to serve their customers.

So as to be able to sell spirits as well as beer, 'Bob' had applied for a victuallers drinks licence in early March 1853 but was refused and was continually refused on an annual basis during his tenure of the premises. In 1855 Elizabeth Fenton of *'The Leather Bottle'*, Garratt Lane and Jane Woodruff of *'The Plough'* in Plough Lane had opposed his application, obviously with a mind to protect their own sales.

However, it was not always bad news in his dealings with the authorities as in May of 1854 Bob had appealed for a reduction of the Poor Rates applied to the property. It had a ground value of £80 and a

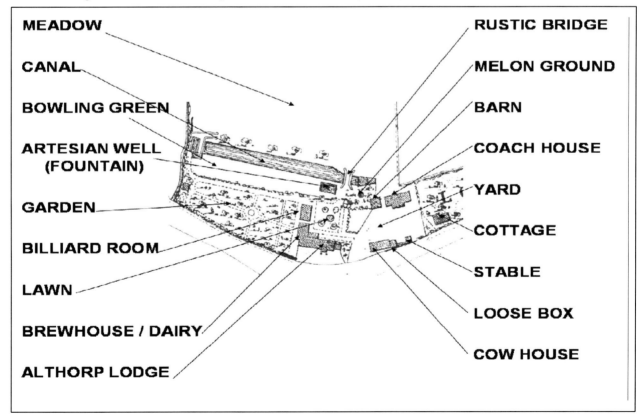

19) A plan of ALTHORP LODGE/THE WELLINGTON INN which shows the gardens and attached buildings. There is a certain amount of guess work used to describe the buildings in the yard next to the Lodge. (Courtesy of Wandsworth Heritage Service).

rateable value of £65. The justices agreed a reduction to be set at £50 and also awarded him costs. They also acted in his favour when granting him a billiard licence in 1856 as he tried to add to the attractions at his premises.

A description of Althorp Lodge in 1856 called it a substantial detached residence and while principally a brick building it had an ornamental composition exterior with a portico at the front and a veranda at the back. On the ground floor there was an entrance lobby with iron balustrades and a mahogany handrail to the staircase, a sitting room with a gothic marble mantle piece and French casements opening out to a greenhouse, a similar room which was used as the bar, had a marble chimney piece, a smaller room communicating, with a scullery adjoining and a stone paved kitchen, a timber and slated building adjoining consisting of a second kitchen, a Brewhouse, a Dairy with slate shelves and galley-tile linings. On the first floor there were three bedrooms, a dressing room another large room with a low ceiling and a water closet. Outside there was a detached Summer, or Billiard room which had a marble chimney piece, ornamental French casements and a sash door, so it was a really substantial and attractive premises.

In the grounds there was a lawn planted with walnut trees and shrubs, a garden stocked with fruit trees, a melon ground with forcing pit and lights, a bowling green and canal, an artesian well in the form of a fountain which also supplied another fountain in the garden which had ornamental rustic bridges, various buildings and a separate meadow.

In the yard there was a three stall stable, a coach house, a loose box with a loft, a lean-to cow house with calf pen, a double-bayed barn with thrashing floor and a cart house.

The land stretching back to Garratt Green comprised almost eight acres in total and the Garratt Lane frontage of the whole property was one hundred and sixty six yards. To relate it to the current numbering on Garratt Lane, it ran from number 737 to number 781. The extent of the grounds behind Althorp Lodge where the pedestrian track was sited, were bounded on the east by Garratt Green and at the sides within the back garden boundaries of the current Franche Court Road to the north and Huntspill Street to the south, neither of which were constructed until after the demise of the running track.

Also in 1856, Bob Sadler appears to have purchased a plot of land fronting on to Garratt Lane to the north of Althorp Lodge. After his tenure at Althorp Lodge, five houses, one with a shop and known as 8-12 Edwards Terrace, had been built very close to the northern side of the lodge and these subsequently became 749-757 Garratt Lane.

20/21) In 1855 Elizabeth Fenton of *'The Leather Bottle'* in Garratt Lane (above) opposed Bob Sadler's application for a victuallers drinks licence as did Jane Woodruff of *'The Plough'* in Plough Lane (below), the building is currently in retail use as a tile shop.

CHAPTER 5
1853
Early events and the controversy of the Tonnawonda Indian

The athletics track Bob created on the land behind Althorp Lodge was originally a roughly square shape. The two longer straights were approximately 200 yards and 160 yards while the shorter sides were approximately 113 yards. This gave a total circuit of 586 yards and meant that three circuits were necessary to achieve a distance of 1 mile. Soon there were regular athletic events held there and some of the best known runners and walkers of the time found their way to the pretty little ground surrounded by fields and set near the pleasant country atmosphere of Bob Sadler's *'Wellington Inn'* with its tea gardens and water features.

The London and South Western railway to Southampton with it's London terminus at Nine Elms until it was extended back to Waterloo Bridge in 1848, ran across Garratt Lane from its opening in 1838 but the *'Earlsfield and Summerstown'* station between Clapham Junction and Wimbledon, which would have greatly assisted anyone travelling to the pedestrian grounds, was not to be built until 1884. It was possible however for spectators using this line to travel on to Wimbledon station and then walk or bus the remaining one and a half miles to Summerstown from there.

It was far more likely that most spectators travelling from central London would have come to *'Wandsworth Town'* station which was on the Richmond Windsor line from Nine Elms and was frequently used by Queen Victoria on her journeys to Windsor, so much so, that the line became known locally as 'Royal'. Opened in 1846, it was purchased by the London and South Western railway the following year and one year later the London terminus was moved back to Waterloo Bridge just like the Southampton line had been. *'Wandsworth Town'* station on this line, initially occupied a site west of North Street not far from the gas works but in 1860 the station was moved to its present site in York Road. Spectators for the pedestrian grounds arriving at this station would either walk the one and three quarter miles down Garratt Lane to Summerstown or be brought down to the ground by horse buses.

During its early life it was variously known as *'The Duke of Wellington New Surrey Grounds'*, *'Garratt Gardens'*, *'Surrey Gardens'*, *'Sadlers Ground'* or *'The Garratt Grounds'* before eventually settling on *'The New Surrey Pedestrian Grounds'* as its proper name. The first event at the new sports venue took place on Easter Monday March 28 1853 exactly one week after the closure of John Garratt's Copenhagen Grounds in Islington, this was a 10 miles race between James Brookson who was a local man from the village of Garratt and James Dawkins of Moorfields and was for £20 a side. The stake money from each man or his backer was deposited to Thomas Wilson the proprietor of one of the main sporting houses for pedestrians, *'The Spotted Dog'* in the Strand. Situated virtually opposite and next to the Strand theatre was the premier sporting newspaper *'Bells Life in London'*, issued on a weekly basis every Sunday and they had suggested that the ground might have been opened a week or two earlier but the delay was possibly caused by Bob Sadler's futile efforts to obtain a licence for Althorp Lodge prior to the opening.

Only a week before the opening, Alfred Badger and George Shaw had been due to race over 880 yards on Wandsworth Common but the event had been prevented from taking place by police intervention. Now however, the provision of a locally enclosed ground for such events would make them more controllable and far less likely to suffer from intervention by the police, who were obviously concerned that large crowds of supporters would be a threat to public order.

On April 24 Bob Sadler came in for some criticism in *'Bells Life'* for not providing results of the various matches held at the ground:-

'We have not received any account of Buxton and Shaw's match on Tuesday last. How is it that the landlord does not make a note of the proceedings at his grounds and forward the same to us for he cannot expect us to send a reporter to every place for minor matches?'

22)CHARLES WESTHALL (1823-1868) gained fame as both a runner and a walker and in 1852 became the first man to run under four and a half minutes for a mile.

Bob was learning the ropes and that to promote the facility properly, he would need to regularly inform the sporting press of activities planned and completed on his grounds.

The very prominent pedestrians thirty year old Charles Westhall and the thirty five year old American George Seward, were two of the most famous athletes of the day to appear at the track as it gained its reputation. In April competing against each other, Westhall won a 400 yards match over 10 hurdles to win a silver cup put up by Bob Sadler and in early August, Seward raced the well known Henry Reed over 440 yards with Reed winning by 4-5 yards in 54 seconds, each man having put up a stake of £50.

Matches were not without controversy. An 880 yards match between Alfred Badger and John Tucker did not happen and Tucker had to forfeit his stake. A 10 miles walking match between 'Old' Smith and James Jones in May ended in argument when Jones was considered to have fouled Smith in the closing stages and the Umpire and Referee were both ordered to attend 'Bells Life' to sort it out. The railing of the course for this event to prevent encroachment was praised in the press and other tracks were urged to adopt this method of containing over excited spectators some who were hell bent on causing trouble. An even bigger controversy occurred when a match between Ben Badger of Wolverhampton and local man James Brookson ended with Badger running alone over the course with Brookson refusing to run having been accused of accepting money to lose the 880 yards race. 'Bell's Life' report on June 19 read:-

23) GEORGE SEWARD (1817-1883) Born in Newhaven, Connecticut, USA, he gained his reputation as an outstanding sprinter in America before coming to England in 1843 and settling in the North East. Later he ran at the Stalybridge Grounds near Manchester and died in Birkenhead.

'This affair at the Surrey Grounds on Monday appears to be enveloped in some degree of mystery. A person of the name of Tonge or Long, who says he backed Brookson, calls upon us to retain his £10, as Brookson would not run. He states that Brookson was keen to give an individual a number of sovereigns to be betted against him. All bets were then declared off, and Brookson would not run. Mr Sadler, the proprietor of the ground, states that there was no race, in consequence of a man named Aldred accusing Brookson of having been offered money to lose the match. Badger ran over the ground at the desire of Brookson, and to claim the stakes, which they say we are to hand over to Badger. They must however come to our office on Wednesday next at one o'clock and explain this matter before we comply with the request'.

On July 3 'Bell's Life' continued with the story:-

'After we had given up the money to Badger on Monday we received a singular epistle, from a lawyer we presume, in which it is stated that he is instructed by James Brookson to apply to us for £10 deposited by him. Why Brookson, when last at our office, desired us to give up the money to Badger!'

Apart from Garratt's James Brookson, another local pedestrian Robert Inwood of Tooting, was involved in a very high profile trial at the Old Bailey. It followed his involvement in a 120 yards race against William Neil of Somers Town held at the Flora Grounds in Bayswater on July 25. Inwood, Neil and two others Frederick Lett and Robert Williams both from Lambeth were indicted for conspiracy. It was claimed that Inwood had signed a document to lose the race but then had 'put the double' on those involved and had won. At the Middlesex Sessions on Monday September 19 when the case was called, neither the prosecutor, believed to be a Mr T Peever, who was either a publican or an oyster-stall keeper, or any witnesses to support the charges were present in the court. After the jury had been sworn in, because there was no evidence in support of the conspiracy charge, verdicts of not guilty were taken and all the defendants freed.

The track in Garratt Lane obviously attracted local men to take up the pedestrian sport. On September 18 'Bell's Life' carried the following announcement:-

'Richard Myford a novice of Garratt, will run for £5 or £10 a side with Shepherd of Wandsworth a mile, Twilley of Wandsworth Common, Adams of Mitcham, Bunyan or Reed of Bermondsey a quarter of a mile. A match can be made any night next week at Mr Sadler's, Duke of Wellington, Garratt Lane, Wandsworth'.

Richard Myford was possibly the son of William Myford who lived at number two Church Street, Summerstown which lay opposite Riverside Drive and 'The Corner Pin' and therefore was living only the short walk across Garratt Lane to the grounds but despite his brave challenge, there is no record of him ever having competed at the Garratt Lane track.

On August 21 'Bells Life' carried an announcement from J F Clarke at The Wellington Club, St James's Street formerly known as Crockford's. Clarke claimed he had just arrived from America with an Indian of the Tonnawands tribe and was prepared to make a match to run 10 miles with William Jackson also known as

The American Deer, or any man in England for any amount of money they cared to name. When the match did come off it was at the Garratt Lane track and would provide the biggest controversy of Bob Sadler's opening year.

William Jackson despite his sobriquet of 'The American Deer' was from Norwich. His birth name had been William Howitt and on Monday October 17 he lined up against 'Black Hawk' promoted as the Tonnawonda Indian from North America and who was rumoured to have run 12 miles within an hour. The match advertised by 'Bells Life' with the heading 'England v USA', attracted some two thousand spectators to pack into the facility despite the inclement rainy weather, for the 4.30 pm start. When the men appeared, Jackson was wearing the normal pedestrian attire while the Indian, sporting long black hair and a moustache, was wearing a pair of nankeen trousers, striped loose shirt and a pair of thin dancing pumps.

From the start it was obvious that the Indian was not a proficient runner and although Jackson allowed him to lead the first lap, it was run at a pathetic pace. Before he had completed a mile Jackson had lapped him and after one further circuit of the track he dropped out altogether allowing Jackson to complete the distance unchallenged.

24) WILLIAM JACKSON, 'The American Deer' (1821-?), was born William Howitt in Norwich. He had a long career as a pedestrian competing at a high level for almost twenty years from the mid 1840's until the early 1860's.

Many of the spectators recognised Black Hawk as a man who actually worked as a crossing sweeper in the vicinity of Moses establishment in New Oxford Street and that he was a native of Calcutta or Bengal. Letters of outrage appeared in the papers from angry spectators denouncing the whole event as an attempt to defraud the public by charging admission under false pretences. Bob Sadler was forced to defend himself and' in an attempt to explain his position he called at "Bell's Life" and handed in the following letter.

'MR EDITOR As the disgraceful scene which took place at my grounds on Monday last is calculated to do me serious injury in my business. I shall feel obliged by your statement of the particulars as far as I know. Jackson called on me personally and asked how much I would give him to run his match with this wonderful Indian at my grounds and as he positively assured me that Mr Beswick had offered him £10 to run at Barking Road. I thought I could not be far wrong in offering £5 although as I stated at the time, it was more than I could afford; however, he did at last accept it. I then made several enquiries respecting this Indian and also his backers; the answer was that he had just been brought over from North America by two military officers and that he was not to be seen or known until the day of the race. The public must be well aware that I never connect myself in any way with sporting matters and that I never lay out a farthing on any race. I believe Jackson to be the sole and only person to blame in the matter. The public will naturally ask the question, how about the gate money? After laying out several pounds in extra fencing to keep out the 'roughs', and £5 to Jackson, I received £4 8s (£4.40), making a loss of several pounds. I can only say in conclusion that I never intend one farthing to be taken at my gate any more, neither will I give the £10 as promised to be run for on Monday next. I do not intend to close the grounds but in future whatever race may come off the public will be admitted free – Yours &c ROBERT SADLER, Oct 18 1853.

Still the controversy raged and the following week Jackson had a letter published in 'Bells Life'.

'Mr Editor: In vindication of my character and as a duty I owe to myself, I beg leave to give the following explanation and reply to the letters which appeared in 'Bell's Life' of last week. I deny having ever seen the Indian previous to our race on the 17th, or knowing anything whatsoever about him, more than the enclosed letter will show and which you will oblige me by publishing, to assure the world that I am innocent of the allegations made against me. I attended at

Crockford's (now the Wellington Dining Rooms,) St James's Street, according to the request made by Mr Linsley therein; and the following is what then occurred. Mr Linsley offered to back an Indian against me for £25 against the Champion's Belt and would allow me to choose the ground, providing it were enclosed, he, (Mr L), to have one third of the gate money, to which I assented. Shortly after this I met Mr Sadler who voluntarily offered to give me £5, and one third of the gate money, if I would run on his grounds. To this I agreed. I now ask the public if I have not a right to make a match with any other 'Black Hawk' or with Mr J Russell, or Levett's friend of twenty years standing, or with Mr Levett himself, or any pretender in pedestrianism, whenever it suits my will, without consulting the public or asking their permission? Though a public man, I am not public property. In reply to the letters that appeared in 'Bell's Life' last week, defaming my character, I feel obliged to such officious friends, who have afforded me great amusement in perusing their epistles at my leisure, for when they are occupied in slandering me they are not injuring others; and as for honesty, which they boast of having so much of, it is a gem of which I profess to have but little, for all boasters are imposters like 'Black Hawk' – I subscribe myself, with all due respect, the public's faithful servant. W JACKSON

"Bell's Life" then added:- The following is Mr Linsley's letter to Jackson alluded to in the above. We give it verbatim et literatim:-

DEAR SIR: I went to see you about a match with an Indian man if you will call any time after 10 o'clock at the Wellington dining rooms at James street and ask for Mr Linsley I will let you know all about it I think it well worth your attending to your ob "Excuse the dirty paper".

(We have now placed the entire of this 'black' affair before the public who doubtless will form a just estimate upon the subject – Ed)

Despite *"Bell's Life"* apparently bringing closure to the correspondence there was a further letter published in their issue of November 6 under the heading JACKSON AND THE (SOI-DISANT) TONNAWONDA INDIAN'S LATE RACE.

MR EDITOR: I must beg leave to apologise for intruding on your valuable time, but, having been alluded to in Mr Jackson's letter of last week, I wish to make a few remarks. With respect to Mr Jackson making matches he has a perfect right to do so with whom he pleases; but when he advertises them to be run in public, the public have an equal right to find fault with and condem an exhibition such as took place on the 17th ult at Garratt Lane, Wandsworth; and as for slandering him, surely writing what really took place cannot be slander. But if Mr J feels so much

amusement in reading these epistles at his leisure, he can have another nut to crack. Who and what is the writer on the dirty bit of paper? Surely at the Wellington he could have had some clean by asking for it. Where were the deposits made and who held the stakes? Perhaps he will feel obliged for these questions; but 'tis his officious slandering friends, as he calls them, and such as them, who will not be imposed on with impunity, that keep bad men a little in order, they fearing that their evil deeds will be exposed. Trusting this will be the last "black" affair Mr Jackson will be engaged in. I am yours, &c, J RUSSELL.

The whole affair showed that it was quite possible to dupe the public by making spurious claims about the potential of a pedestrian without him ever having to demonstrate his athletic powers. It was also interesting to discover that appearance money to attract prominent pedestrians was already in vogue. Anxious to preserve his reputation, Sadler's offer to give free admission for future events showed that he felt he could still make a profit from beer sales at his Wellington Inn and perhaps other attractions in the grounds, without the gate money income. The appearance of an Indian had proved an exotic and irresistible attraction for the Victorian public but they were not prepared to be enticed out of their hard earned money if the contest was not considered to be above board and contested by genuine pedestrians of some calibre. Some years later a similarly irresistible occasion involving a true native American would be promoted at the Garratt Lane facility and William Jackson was also to figure prominently again at Garratt Lane, both on the track and in the County Court.

Free entry to the facility attracted over a thousand spectators for a 100 yards race the following week between Edwin Reed and James Bunyan when Reed appears to have had his trousers, shoes and handkerchief stolen while he was running. On the last day of October James Stainer and William Priestley contested a 1 mile race and a crowd of one and a half thousand was the estimated attendance to see Stainer win by 30 yards in a time of 4:50 and even intensely cold weather on Boxing Day did not deter over two thousand coming to witness a variety of running and walking contests.

By the end of 1853 almost forty events had taken place at the new facility. Robert Sadler, although having come in for some criticism, had put the venue firmly on the sporting map. It had attracted large crowds to the little hamlets of Garratt and Summerstown and it must have been good for local businesses, some local men had tested their skill and ability in various contests and the Garratt Lane facility had become an accepted venue for pedestrianism in London.

CHAPTER 6
1854-1855
More controversy and a tragedy for 'The American Deer'

Some details of the pedestrian sport seem very strange to us today when races are all started by an appointed official. It was quite common in the middle of the nineteenth century for competitors to arrange to have a 'mutually agreed start' where they would feign and feint against each other until they would both reach agreement on the start having been fair and continue the race on to its conclusion. One such start took place on March 6 1854 where Edward Grover and Edwin Reed, matched to run 120 yards for £10 a side, spent over an hour on the start line before the race really started and resulted in a win for Grover. Delays such as this must have exasperated spectators and obviously delayed other events that were to follow. Such was the case on this foggy Monday evening and after another couple of races, a proposed 2 miles walking match between James Hilliard and William Taylor, which had already been postponed from February 20 due to a disagreement about the officials, was postponed this time because of the failing light, or was it? Another reporter suggested that the match had started with a 'non-appointed' referee who had left the ground before the completion of the race. Yet another letter to *'Bell's Life'* came from J Chapman claiming that he was the referee and that Hilliard had won by thirty yards or more finishing in complete darkness. *"Bell's Life"* described it as *'a mysterious affair'* and suggested the parties concerned meet at their office at 1.00 pm on Monday March 13 to ascertain what really took place and to resolve the problem. The eventual decision announced in *'Bell's Life'* on March 19 was that *'In accordance with the decision of the referee, the stakes in this walking match has been handed over to Hilliard'*.

Advertised race start times were rarely adhered to and some races were even advertised to take place between say 2 and 4 pm. Also, because of the mutually agree start rule being prevalent, it would have been very difficult for spectators to know when to arrive at the venue and they would certainly have no idea when they would leave. It would be some time before starts would always be made by the report of a gun fired by a designated starter.

With an easterly wind being the cause of a bitterly cold Easter Monday, a crowd of over 2000 descended on the Garratt Lane ground but had to wait for over an hour for Edwin Groves and Daniel Welsh to start their 120 yards race for £25 a side. *'Bell's Life'* reported that *'Welsh repeatedly asked his opponent to walk to the scratch and start, which, however, he did not by any means appear inclined to do'*. When they eventually did get away the race was so close that the referee gave his decision as a dead heat. *'Bell's Life'*

declared:- *'The pedestrians must therefore run again, or draw their money'*. The match was rearranged and on May 15 they met again on a section of level road near Slough. Once again they spent the best part of an hour dodging at the start line and eventually the police intervened and stopped the event taking place at all. *'Bell's Life'* made the amusing comment:- *'Should these men meet to run again, we would suggest the selection of the longest day in the year and to be at scratch by daybreak'*. However, a third meeting did happen but this time at South Mimms, for an increased stake of £40 a side and Thomas Dell the referee gave the very close decision to Groves by half a yard.

On May Day Walter Hatley and James Hilliard had a 4 miles walk arranged for £10 a side at Garratt Lane but they and their backers on failing to agree on a referee and umpires, the event did not take place. This match also was rearranged and took place between the 22nd and 24th milestones on the Oxford Road near Slough. By the end of the third mile Hilliard was 200 yards ahead and Hatley, finding he had no chance gave in and so crest-fallen was he that he could not keep from crying.

Many match decisions and results were disputed and *"Bell's Life"* often tried to sort out the mess. In late May they felt moved to publish the following:- *'Our time has been too much occupied this week to even read the pros and cons relative to disputed matches and there much in some instances be great disreputability among certain parties for scarcely any two accounts agree'*.

It seems very strange that a large gap then appears in events taking place at the Garratt Lane ground. Apart from a 100 yards race in November 1854 between two young men named Fisher and Brown, nothing appears to have happened at the venue between early May 1854 and Easter Monday April 9 1855. It can only be guessed at as to why this gap appeared and maybe it was due to illness in the Sadler family. Despite this inactivity at Garratt Lane, pedestrianism flourished all over the country but was not without its problems. In October 1854 *'Bell's Life'* made this announcement to their readers:-

'Mr O'Grady, who for a long period constructed, with Assistants, the Pedestrian, Trotting, Pigeon Shooting, Nurr and Spell, Quoiting and other departments of this journal, has been removed from all connection with this establishment. It was not until the 14th instant that we were made acquainted with the suspicions to which we had been exposed through the misappropriation, by Mr O'Grady (in whom, up to that time, we had placed implicit confidence), of a great

number of checks (sic) entrusted to him for the purpose of paying stakes, when we took immediate steps for his removal. It is requested that in future all communications may be addressed to the Editor and that any complaints may be forwarded without delay to Messrs Clement Brothers, the proprietors of 'Bell's Life' in London'.

It appears that various matches had been arranged and publicised and then had not taken place, one of these was a 3 miles race at Garratt Lane planned for Friday December 22 1854. It is not clear how a cancelled event could benefit the participants but certainly two men racing against each other on a regular basis could come to mutual agreement as to the outcome and thereby benefit those who were privy to this information.

William Howitt better known as William Jackson or 'The American Deer,' having retired from pedestrianism and set up in business investing all his money in the erection of a nursery and cucumber houses in the vicinity of Norbiton, lost everything in a disastrous fire on December 7 and as the premises were uninsured, unfortunately he lost everything he had accumulated from his years of pedestrianism. This tragedy forced him to return to the sport and he would be seen again in the Garratt Lane track despite his dispute with Bob Sadler regarding his race with 'Black Hawk' in October 1853.

"Bell's Life" also had a problem with the prominent Marylebone pedestrians Charles Cook and James Stainer. On March 18 1855 they wrote:-

'The two mile match between these men turns out to have been a premeditated piece of roguery alike discreditable to both parties. We have scarcely patience to record our disgust at such proceedings and their very frequent occurrence must eventually tend to scare all supporters of pedestrianism. We shall return each man his stake on personal application to our office on Thursday next at twelve o'clock. All bets are off. In the following week's edition they commented:- After a further investigation of this affair in the presence of both parties, we have determined that the stakes shall go according to the award of the referee. Stainer on his first calling at this office, and producing the document which fully established his own guilt, gave us to understand that Cook's participation in the 'sell' could be made equally

clear. This however, he subsequently failed in doing: and we now can only have the satisfaction of knowing that one at least who has done wrong has not met with success. We refrain from giving any opinion about Cook. He can receive the money on Wednesday at twelve o'clock at our office'.

If, for whatever reason, the Garratt Lane Grounds had virtually closed for 11 months, it certainly re-opened with a huge event when a 10 miles handicap race was arranged for Easter Monday April 9 1855 between two of the biggest names in pedestrianism, James Pudney of Mile End, the current 10 miles champion of England and John Levett from Battersea who had run the distance in the fastest known time of 51:45 but now with the appearance of James Pudney on the scene was providing the first serious competition for Levett.

25) Battersea born JOHN LEVETT (1826-1876) held the British 10 miles record of 51:45 for 33 years and also set a record of 11 miles 350 yards for the greatest distance completed in one hour. He spent much of his later life in Dublin.

John Levett had first seen the light of day in Battersea on June 1 1826. A profile of him in the 'Illustrated Sporting News' stated that his first run had been at 'The Red House' grounds in Battersea Fields aged fifteen months when he covered two yards and that his first race for money was over 100 yards which he won. However, we do know that he won a 1 mile contest on Wandsworth Common in January 1848 and that by 1852, he had become one of England's leading pedestrians. At John Garratt's Old Cope ground in Islington he won the first 10 miles champion belt race against George Frost in a British record of 52:35. In a second defence of the belt against William Jackson on the same track, he again won, setting a new British record of 51:45 that was to last for 33 years. Two years later in Liverpool, he set a 1 Hour running record when he covered 11 miles 350 yards in the allotted sixty minutes.

Some four years older than Pudney, Levett would receive a 200 yards start. The contest, for £50 a side, attracted over 2000 spectators to Sadler's ground for a 5.00 pm start. About an hour late the contest got underway but Pudney was well below form and unable to close the 200 yards allowance given to Levett. Pudney decided to give up the contest at the start of the seventh mile and Levett went on to complete the distance without opposition for an easy victory and take the £100 prize. Pudney immediately issued a challenge to Levett for a race over 6 miles for

£50 a side with Levett to receive 100 yards allowance and a date was agreed of May 14 for them to be back at the Garratt Lane track.

In the lead up to the event it was said that Levett was confident enough to be willing to wager his share of the gate money with Pudney or his friends on the result. Despite it being the merry month of May, the weather was cold and bleak and it could not have pleased those gathered that the race, which had been advertised for a 3.00 pm start was delayed until nearly 6.00 pm. apparently in an effort to entice more people into the ground. Both men set off at a cracking pace and it was not until the middle of the fourth mile that Pudney made up the 100 yards handicap and overtook Levett. The Battersea man was far from finished however and in the remaining laps the lead changed hands frequently. It was not until the final half mile that Pudney made the race his and finished in 32 minutes 10 seconds some forty yards ahead of Levett. Both men had run themselves to exhaustion and had to be assisted from the track to their changing room.

These two big Pudney v Levett races had really put Garratt Lane back on the pedestrian map after the previous year of inactivity and Bob Sadler announced that he would provide a belt worth £25 to be raced for in a 10 miles handicap on Whit Monday May 28 hoping to attract some big names. 'Bell's Life' praised his efforts:- 'There is little doubt that a large attendance will repay the exertions of the landlord, who has been at much trouble and expense in making a small ground very serviceable'.

Unfortunately for Sadler, poor weather on the day prevented a good attendance and although seventeen had entered. only seven showed up to contest the prizes of the belt and £5 for first place, with £3, £1. 10s (£1.50) and 10/6 (52 1/2p) going for the lesser places. The men were set around the track

26) JAMES PUDNEY (1830-1897) was born in Lambeth but lived mostly in the east end of London and was usually described as being from Mile End. For a time he was the 10 miles champion and while he was still competing regularly was the proprietor of the well known sporting public house 'The Coach and Horses' in Back Church Lane, Whitechapel.

with their various allowances with only Pudney having to run the full 10 miles. By five miles only Pudney, Levett Cook and Priestley were left in contention. Cook and Priestley had received a 400 yards start and Levett 150 yards. Priestley dropped away but Pudney and Levett continued to try and break down Cook's lead. Although Pudney got close enough to challenge for the lead, on every occasion he did so, Cook spurted away and eventually came in the winner by some 300 yards having run the 10 miles, less his 400 yards start, in a very creditable 53 minutes 20 seconds with Pudney, Levett and Priestley claiming the minor prizes.

The following evening, John Buxton and Joseph Lynch contested a 20 miles walk which would have required them to complete 60 laps of the track and it only attracted a small attendance at the ground. Lynch failed to complete the distance but Buxton strode to victory in three hours sixteen minutes.

Numerous other pedestrian events regularly took place on venues in and around London with the other main centres of the sport being Manchester, Sheffield and Birmingham. Side by side with big plans for big events on enclosed grounds, smaller events regularly took place locally and quite often on the public roads. Cromwell of Sydenham and John Reid of Norwood were matched to run 150 yards for £10 a side on the Croydon Road, Westow Hill, Norwood and 'A Novice' wagered that he could walk 6 miles within the hour for £5 a side on the Kennington Road while a 150 yards race took place between George Watson and Henry Fisher on Mitcham Green although it is not clear if this was the Fair Green or the Cricket Green.

Events continued on a weekly basis at Sadler's ground. Towards the end of June a 7 miles walk between Frank Diamond and William Newman, despite pleasant weather, attracted less than 50 spectators and the condition of the track and the arrangements for the pedestrians comfort caused 'Bell's Life' to criticise Bob Sadler. On July 7 they wrote:-

'We cannot but observe that the course was by no means in good condition. We walked over it and found it in several places uneven and strewed abundantly with stones of a large size: if Mr Sadler wishes pedestrians to nominate his ground for their matches to come off at, he surely should consult their feelings a little more; their comfort he also appears to take very little trouble about, as the only place assigned to pedestrians to strip and arrange their toilets is in a stable! This is decidedly not as it ought to be and we would recommend Mr Sadler to see that this be remedied in future, his premises being sufficiently extensive to afford the temporary use of a room'.

Further criticism came his way when the promised start time of 5 o'clock was not adhered to and it was 6:26 pm before the race commenced. Pedestrians Hotine and Stainer were appointed the umpires and Buxton and another novice pedestrian acted as 'equerries' for the walkers providing them with drinks or anything else they required. 'Bell's Life' noted that the pedestrians were in conversation with each other during the second mile and 'a looker-on would never for a moment imagine that they were pitted against each other for the large sum of £50'. The contest progressed with both men always in close contact alternating the lead until the last of the twenty one laps when they began to race each other in earnest with Diamond just crossing the finishing line a yard or so in front and immediately collapsed through exhaustion having walked the 7 miles in 56 minutes 50 seconds.

There were further problems for Bob Sadler and poor publicity for the track a week later when Henry Fisher and John Wray met to contest a 120 yards handicap. The men spent two hours twenty minutes at the scratch line with upwards of 30 false starts without racing. In disgust the appointed referee left the ground. They subsequently signed fresh articles to hold the event the following week and if the 'mutual consent' start method failed again, then after half an hour the race would be started by the report of a pistol.

Despite incessant rain over 1000 spectators arrived at the track on Monday July 16 primarily to watch a match between William Jackson 'The American Deer' and George Frost 'The Suffolk Stag'. They were disappointed however as although Jackson arrived in good time, Frost did not appear. He did subsequently offer Jackson £3 for his inconvenience and apologised that illness had been the cause of his absence. The following Monday, Richard Manks and John Levett both failed to appear for an advertised 20 miles match

and to add to the disappointment of the assembled crowd, they had to endure torrential rain. James Hilliard and Nathaniel Field did not run their advertised 1 mile matches Field had only paid ten shillings (50p) of his £5 stake. 'Bell's Life' was scathing:-

'Those gentlemen who wait upon us, and wish us to proclaim (in print) to the world, that on such and such a day, at such and such a place, they intend to exhibit their ambulatory or curricular powers, have much to answer for when they break the word of promise so shamefully as they have of late...........This is breaking faith with the public in a manner that we cannot too severely condemn and if repeated must tend materially to disgust the heretofore patrons and supporters of pedestrianism'

At least for once their criticism was aimed at the pedestrians and not directly aimed at Bob Sadler.

James Pudney was still smarting from his defeat by Charles Cook in the 10 miles handicap race held on May 28. A return race was arranged for the Garratt Lane ground with Cook once again to receive a 400 yards start. There was great excitement in the little villages of Garratt and Summerstown on Monday July 30 as close to 4,000 assembled in the ground for a 5.00 pm start in very fine weather. The far more famous 25 year old Pudney was prepared to stake £25 against the 19 year old Cook's stake of £15 and the belt he had won in the previous race. The pedestrian James Stainer acted as starter and a throw of his cap into the air was the signal for the men to begin their race. Pudney's first task was to cut back on the 400 yards advantage he had allowed Cook and this he immediately began to do. By the end of the fifth mile he had managed to reduce the lead to 150 yards but then to the amazement and disappointment of the crowd, at the corner which completed the fifth mile. he stopped short as if he had been seized with cramp and gave up. It was only left for Cook to run rather leisurely over the last 5 miles and completed the 10 miles, minus of course his 400 yards start, in 64 minutes. Despite the disappointment, the race did at least restore a measure of respectability to the track.

However, only a week later the track came in for more criticism. Although a number of handicap races had been arranged for Monday August 6 which had attracted 1000 spectators, the start time of half past two was insufficient to allow all the races to be completed because of the approaching darkness. Five heats of a 150 yards handicap were completed as were three heats of a 1 mile handicap but the finals had to be held over until the following day. Some of the runners who had been attracted by the prizes of £10, £3 and £1 for first, second and third places had travelled long distances to support the events and now would incur the extra expense of an overnight stay to add to their costs. The very prominent pedestrian Henry Reed felt moved to show his disgust in a letter to *'Bell's Life'* he complained about his treatment in his heat of the 150 yards:-

'The person who advertised the prizes had four or five of his own men entered and they were determined that no one else should win. I caught all the men in my lot at about 80 yards and tried to get by them but they would not let me. I tried first on one side and then the other and then the middle of the ground but it was of no use for as soon as I came to their shoulder they crossed me and shut me out. Now sir, handicaps in or near London have always been looked on with suspicion and this will not tend to raise them, for almost everyone on the ground expressed their disgust at the proceedings. Yours &c H A Reed'.

This letter prompted a response from George Phillips the following week:-

'MR EDITOR: I am surprised that H A Reed should complain of bad treatment in the late Garratt Lane handicaps when he was solely the cause of it and I am the innocent sufferer by being thrown violently down by him. He had no right on the side of the course on which I ran as many persons present are ready to testify. I have been laid up and prevented from attending my business and am likely to continue so (by the testimony of my medical advisor) for at least a month by a fractured collar bone and as I had no other intention than that of winning, I flatly deny his accusation on the part of myself of being employed to jostle him. In conclusion, I beg to say (as he boasts of catching the men at 80 yards) that I will take the 12 yards start of him in 100 at the coming-in end, when I shall not be able to touch him, for £5 or £10. I cannot find more money as I am only a working lad. I am, GEO PHILLIPS'.

Despite these exchanges between the men and the serious injury to Phillips, the referee for the race had seen no need to intervene on behalf of either runner.

Fine weather on the Monday followed by heavy rain on the Tuesday which reduced the spectators to 50 or 60, added to the misery as did a further complaint from *'The American Deer'* William Jackson who objected to *'Friend of Norwich'* competing under an assumed name in the mile handicap and when it was discovered that the man's name was actually John Brighton he was disqualified for using a false name and the £10 prize awarded to Charles Cook. On the Tuesday, despite five men having qualified for the 150 yards final, only Harry Margetts and Daniel Welsh contested the race and Margetts won a close contest by a yard.

In the next three weeks of August the Monday fare provided at the ground saw contests featuring very prominent pedestrians. On August 13 Henry Reed and Thomas Horspool of Sheffield raced over 880 yards for £50 a side. The postponed match, between William Jackson and George Frost for £25 a side was scheduled for August 20 and on August 27 a field of celebrated runners gathered for a 10 miles handicap, prizes for which had been offered by W Sadler of Garratt Lane who was presumably William, Bob Sadler's brother. Entrance fee for the race was two shillings and sixpence (12½p) and if accepted a further two and sixpence (12½p) would be payable. The advertising also stipulated that runners must declare the colours they would compete in.

The Henry Reed versus Thomas Horspool clash was eagerly anticipated as the two had run a similar contest at Halifax in April 1854 which had resulted in a win for Reed by two yards in the very fast time of 1 minute 58 seconds. By 1858 Horspool would become the fastest miler in Britain with a 4:23.0 record performance in Manchester. The betting was at evens as it was considered both men were well matched. At five minutes past 7.00 pm the race began and Horspool went into an immediate lead which he increased throughout to come in an easy winner by 25 to 30 yards in a time of 2 minutes 3 seconds. Many present were very surprised that Reed should have been so easily beaten.

The rearranged 5 miles match between William Jackson *'The American Deer'* and George Frost *'The Suffolk Stag'* did not draw a large attendance. It was perhaps thought that although these men were at the forefront of pedestrianism that they were both past their best. Jackson's running career had started some fifteen years earlier and having already retired once, had only returned to the sport to try and recoup some of the massive losses he had sustained in the Norbiton fire of 1854. Frost, although younger, was said to look *'haggard and careworn'* and *'presenting not a vestige of that elasticity and agility which so characterised him but a few years since in all his matches'*. The little betting that took place was at evens. Bill Price officiated as Jackson's helper while local Wandsworth pedestrian William Shepherd acted in a similar capacity for Frost. The race began at 5.45 pm and both men dashed off Frost leading by nine or ten yards through the first mile in 5:35. During the second mile, they alternated the lead but Jackson led at the 2 miles post and continued to increase his lead. By the third stretch of the last lap of the fourth mile, Frost called a halt and left Jackson to complete the distance unchallenged in a time of 26:29.

Bob Sadler was obviously anxious to improve the standard of events at his track and he felt the need to contact *'Bell's Life'* to request they state that:-

'In future, no foot race will on any pretence, be allowed in his grounds for a sum less than £5 a side

and that the money must in every case be staked at the office of 'Bell's Life'.

While printing his request, the editor took the opportunity to recommend to him that if he wished to raise pedestrianism in the favour of the public that he should take measures to ensure punctuality in the starting of races.

The great 10 miles handicap race on August 27 had attracted an entry of ten well known pedestrians and it was a pity that six of them, Pudney, Frost, Bunn, Friend, Shepperd and Fromour had withdrawn leaving only William Jackson, John Levett, Charles Cook and William Newman to race for Sadler's £15 first prize with £5 going to the second finisher and the entry money to be divided amongst the others. The recent request for punctual starts by *'Bell's Life'* seemed to have fallen on deaf ears as the printed handbills for the event had clearly stated that the race would come off at 4 o'clock precisely and it was fully two hours later that the men made their appearance. Levett was placed on the scratch mark with Cook having a 50 yards start, Jackson 100 and Newman 250. Although the weather was fine, less than 200 spectators had been attracted to the event and in their betting favoured Jackson, his win the previous week against Frost being fresh in their minds. During the third mile Levett had caught all the others and the four men ran as a group for the next few laps and the half way mark was passed in 26:20. During the seventh mile Cook turned his ankle, later claiming it had been caused by a loose stone, and left the race to the other three. Newman began to be dropped in the ninth mile and the final mile was contested just by Jackson and Levett. With only fifty yards remaining they were neck and neck but Levett made a sudden rush and came home about eight yards in front in a time of 54:08. *'Bell's Life'* however casted some aspersions on the result as they were not totally convinced that Jackson had exerted himself to his fullest extent in that final lap.

Yet more criticism came Sadler's way at the end of September when he had offered a silver watch as the prize in a 4 miles walking event for men who had never won above £5 in a match. *'Bell's Life'* reported:-

'With regard to the arrangements for this match, we must say nothing could possibly be worse. For a long time we thought there was no referee on the ground, at length a person was pointed out to us whom we were told held that office but as far as our observations went he by no means paid that attention to the match that such a functionary should, and the consequence was that the competitors walked or ran just as they pleased. The upshot however of the affair was that after a ludicrous melange of walking, trotting, running and every other species of pedestrial movement, it was generally admitted that Jenns walked fairer (!) than any of the others and Mr Sadler decided on giving him the watch'.

Also, Clarke, one of the competitors for the watch complained bitterly to *'Bell's Life'* of the gross mismanagement of the affair and declared that when he asked the referee who had won the match, he told him that he did not know. The final comment from Bell's editor was:-

'We strongly recommend Mr Sadler, if he wishes his grounds to be patronised by the public, to have matters better arranged in future'.

A large crowd was attracted to Garratt Lane on Monday November 26 for the third meeting between Charles Cook of Marylebone and James Pudney of Mile End over 10 miles. On Whit Monday Cook had been the surprise winner of a 10 miles handicap running from a 400 yards start and at the end of July, over the same distance and with the same allowance for Cook, Pudney had retired at half way claiming injury. Now came the third meeting and on this occasion Cook was only allowed a 200 yards advantage. The gun was fired for the race to get underway at 3.40 pm and Pudney set about his task of reducing Cook's lead. At a rate of about forty yards per mile he steadily eat into the advantage and by the end of the sixth mile passed in 31:40 he was within a few yards of his rival. In the seventh mile he passed him and gradually increased his advantage to the finish achieved in 53:30 with Cook coming home about 50 yards adrift. Despite the fast time, many observers though that over the last five miles, Pudney had not run at the top of his speed. In those days it was sufficient to gain victory and win the prize and not so much emphasis was put on the time achieved. Also of course, for a top pedestrian to show his full capabilities would not be beneficial in future handicap races as it would only increase the advantage he would be expected to allow his competitors.

Cook was back at Garratt Lane on Christmas Eve for a 6 miles handicap against William Jackson when he would receive 100 yards start and there would also be a I mile handicap event for novices who had never won £5 held on the same evening for which Bob Sadler had put up a silver snuff box as the prize for the winner and those wishing to view the snuff box in advance could do so at Mr Wilson's *'Spotted Dog'* in the Strand. One interested spectator on the evening was the Spanish pedestrian Antonio Genaro who had signed articles to compete against George Frost in a 4 hours race to take place at the Garratt Lane ground two days later. Jackson and Cook got away at 4.00 pm on heavy ground due to the sudden thaw in the frosty weather. By the end of the third mile Jackson had eaten away Cook's 100 yards lead and went on to win by some twenty yards in 33:30 and Bob Sadler's silver snuff box went to Andrews of Holborn who won the Novices 1 mile race in 5:20.

CHAPTER 7
1856
A flamboyant Spaniard and Mr Armfield's mare Polly

The 4 Hours race due for December 26 had to be postponed due to the indisposition of the gentleman appointed as referee and was rearranged to take place on the following Tuesday New Year's Day and for whatever reason it was attended by a much smaller crowd than had been expected. Antonio Genaro had become famous for long distance racing against horses at Longchamps in France. He was 32 years old, 5 feet 5 inches in height and weighed in at ten stones four pounds while George Frost, who had long been considered one of England's leading pedestrians, was 30, five feet six and a half inches tall and weighed only eight stone. The agreed terms, apart from the wager of £25 a side, were for the runners to run for 4 hours unceasingly and for the man running the greatest distance in that time to win. If either runner was reduced to walking he would immediately be disqualified. The agreed start time was 12.00 Noon and for once it was properly observed.

About ten minutes before the start time both men appeared. Frost had a woollen wrapper around his shoulders while Genaro cut a more dashing figure shrouded in a Spanish cloak and smoking a cigar!!!. On his head he wore a blue foraging cap on which was embroidered in gold lettering in Spanish which read 'Genaro, the Spanish runner' above this lettering

there was also embroidered a Spanish crown. As the start time approached this cap was laid aside and replaced with a blue velvet cap with a large pink rosette on one side and a plume of feathers. When he removed his cloak it was seen that he wore a light blue silk jacket and trousers, slashed and bound with white and adorned with innumerable rows of small buttons and in addition he had a satin scarf loosely cast around his shoulders. The good people assembled in this small hamlet of Wandsworth must have viewed the scene before them with a mixture of disbelief, mirth and astonishment.

The race got underway at exactly noon and Frost immediately went into the lead, Genaro surprising the watchers with his very short and rapid stride which they had not expected. They were also surprised that Genaro decided to run with his hands in the pockets of his trousers for the whole of the first lap. By the end of the first mile, Frost led by 20 yards which he had increased to 300 yards by the fifth mile. It looked likely that Genaro would be lapped but during the eighth mile Frost informed those watching that he was experiencing rheumatic pains and he was running with some difficulty. By the end of the ninth mile Genaro had reduced his lead to 80 yards with Frost recording 59:47 to Genaro's 60:02 and by 10 miles they were shoulder to shoulder in 67:15. Genaro now

27) GEORGE FROST *'The Suffolk Stag'* **during a race for the 10 miles Championship Belt donated by John Garratt at The Copenhagen Grounds, Islington, in January 1852.**

tracked close behind Frost for the next few laps but made no attempt to pass him. In the twelfth mile, Frost shouted to the stand that he was 'All right again', and proceeded to increase his lead so that by the start of the thirteenth mile he was 100 yards ahead. Genaro began to show some signs of distress and on the first lap of the fourteenth mile Frost lapped him and continued to increase the pace and soon was a lap and a half ahead. As Genaro came to the end of his fourteenth mile Genaro looked deathly pale and decided to call a halt. Frost continued to the end of his lap and was stopped by the referee as Genaro's finish had given Frost the victory only having run for one hour thirty eight minutes and two seconds to win a four hour race.

It had been a colourful spectacle for the people of Garratt and Summerstown but it was slightly marred by a degree of trouble caused by a section of the crowd, perhaps fuelled by Bob Sadler's beer, who swarmed around Genaro's carriage in Garratt Lane as he prepared to return to London, shouting and insulting him with bad language and suggesting he accept their challenges to run against him. 'Bell's Life' commented:-

'Such conduct was unmanly, ungenerous and above all decidedly un-English but so true it is that a live ass may kick with impunity at a dead lion. We blushed for our countrymen and sincerely hope we shall never again witness a repetition of such blackguard behaviour'.

Events continued at the ground on a regular basis. Despite the intensely cold weather four to five hundred spectators were attracted there for a 4 miles handicap and a 1 mile novice's race on February 18. Charles Cook carried off the gold watch prize in the 4 miles race beating prominent men James Pudney, John Syddall, Charles Westhall, William Jackson and William Newman into the bargain and Jeremiah Mahoney won the silver one for his victory in the novice's 1 mile. Bob Sadler received credit for the condition of the facility and the fact that the track had been well rolled. Prior to the event and to attract entries, the prize watches had been on display at Mr Wilson's 'Spotted Dog' in the Strand which was perhaps the main sporting public house in London for the sport of Pedestrianism.

Some strange events were sometimes planned but did not always materialise. A Mr Armfield challenged Charles Cook to race him 2 miles over sixty hurdles 3 feet 6 inches high with the main difference being that Mr Armfield would be sitting astride his horse Polly. The event was planned for March 17 but Cook had to pull out and forfeit his stake because he was due to race a 10 miles event four days later so the Garratt Lane event was rescheduled for the end of the month.

Some very convoluted challenges were issued in the pages of 'Bell's Life' such as:-

'James Stainer of Marylebone will run James Mahoney of Bermondsey half a mile or one mile level, or his brother can have the start he asked for at Wandsworth; or Stainer will run Andrews of Holborn and give him a small start in one mile or he will run C Cook of Marylebone half a mile or a mile level for from £5 to £15 a side; or Groves 100 yards if he will give five yards start; or will take three yards in 100 from Preston; or run H Fisher 200 yards level for from £5 to £15 a side; or any man in Marylebone from 100 to 440 yards level on the same terms'.

So, within a few lines, Stainer had challenged six men by name and the whole of the male population of Marylebone. He would then sit back and wait for a response which once again would be through the medium of 'Bell's Life'. Articles would then be drawn up to be signed and deposits for the agreed sums of money would be made at allotted places usually public houses or 'Bell's Life'.

Other local communities were always willing to stage events to attract the local population. In the pretty little village of Sutton a 100 yards race had been arranged between a well known sporting personality known as Mr C B and the publican of 'The Angel Hotel' known as George. The event possibly took place on the roadway near the pub and although George took an early lead one of his feet tripped on the rough surface and he fell. It was recorded that his amiable better half eased his bruised shoulder by well rubbing in some brandy and opodeldoc.

Nearly 2000 spectators made their way to Garratt Lane for the long pending 1 mile race that was to take place between Mile End's James Pudney and Birmingham's William Wallace on Monday March 10 for stakes of £25 a side but Bob Sadler again received criticism for his lack of preparation of the track. Wallace took an early lead but was soon overtaken by Pudney who piled on the pace. At the end of the second of the three laps Pudney led by 15 yards and Wallace having been run off his feet resigned the contest. His backers were very disappointed as their man had apparently done extraordinary times in his training.

Good Friday fell on March 21 and over a thousand were in attendance to see the local man from Garratt James Brookson return to the track following a break of some years. He was matched in a 10 miles handicap against Charles Cook for £10 a side and would be allowed a one minute start. Brookson was now 32 and was some eleven years younger than Cook but had resumed his training in readiness for the event. Both men appeared in their running costumes in time for the scheduled 4.30 pm start. When the signal was given, Brookson charged off and had covered some 300 yards before Cook was allowed to start a minute behind. After some 4 miles Cook began to eat into Brookson's lead and by the ninth mile was within 120 yards, before the finish he had closed to within 50 yards but gained no more as Brookson's long lurching strides took him to victory in 55:35.

The Easter holiday fare continued with an event on the programme for the Monday sports styled as The All-England 880 yards handicap which was to be run in the form of three heats with the winners to contest a final race for three prizes of £7.10.0 (£7.50), £2 and 10/- (50p). It was estimated that about twelve hundred were in attendance and were enjoying the fine weather. The course was in good condition but the meeting was held under the management of Bill Price who surprisingly had neglected to appoint any umpires or a referee. As there had been a dead heat in the third round and both men were allowed into the final, .there were four men contesting it. The main prize was carried off by James Pudney who showed his wide range of ability by leading home Harry Margetts, Daniel Welsh and James Stainer. This promotion at Garratt Lane had come in for some fairly local competition with the opening on the very same day of the Lord Auckland Racing Grounds attached to *'The Lord Auckland'*

28) A poster advertising a varied bill of fare on offer at The Red House, Battersea Fields.

tavern in Falcon Road Battersea. The public house had no doubt been named after the popular Lord who had been vicar of Battersea from 1835 to 1847.

The formation and laying out of Battersea Park in 1853 had led to the closure of the popular sporting facility in Battersea Fields known as *'The Red House'*, a tavern which lay close to the present Chelsea Bridge and where the proprietor was James Ireland. The grounds behind the public house of approximately 120 square yards had been a venue for a variety of different sporting events including such entertainment as horse racing, donkey racing, boxing, wrestling, ballet, tight-rope, quoits, putting the stone, tossing the caber, throwing the hammer, fencing, broadsword, running, walking and pigeon shooting. The shooting of live wild birds would certainly be banned today but at that time sportsmen could buy pigeons at fifteen shillings (75p) a dozen, starlings at four shillings (20p) and sparrows at two shillings 2/- (10p). Organised shooting parties would then take place to determine the best shot. On August 30 1852 John Garratt had been backed to travel down the Thames from Vauxhall Bridge in a tub drawn by four geese starting at 3.00 pm and to land at *'The Red House'*. Whether the wager had been achieved and if the John Garratt was the same man who had managed the Copenhagen Grounds in Islington and would later be prominent in Wandsworth, is unclear.

Following the closure of *'The Red House'*, a local publican William Cockell had set up an alternative pigeon shooting and rabbit coursing ground with facilities for quoits and other games behind his public house *'The Lord Auckland'* in Falcon Road, Battersea. He had now decided to add a running track for pedestrians and he advertised it as being of easy access, situated within one mile of Battersea Bridge and within five minutes walk of Clapham station. While Cockell was the proprietor, the manager of the track would be the famous pedestrian Charles Westhall.

Like Garratt Lane, this would be an enclosed ground behind a public house and would be roped and staked to restrict access to the track which was an oblong shape measuring 441 yards and the intention was to increase its distance and erect a stand to house 300 people by Whitsuntide. Mr Cockell claimed he had fourteen rooms that he would be prepared to make available for pedestrians to strip and dress in. This particular luxury was one facility that had always been complained about at Bob Sadler's Garratt Lane track. On the opening day of the new track, Westhall himself won a silver watch to add to his collection with a victory in the 4 miles walking handicap. Although the facility initially flourished and attracted large entries for the events it promoted, its life was short lived and it was closed down early in 1857 after only ten months of life.

The long talked of match between Charles Cook the Marylebone pedestrian and Mr Armfield's mare to race 2 miles and jump 60 hurdles with Cook to receive a one minute start attracted about a thousand spectators to Garratt Lane on March 31. Running outside the ropes which bounded the track, Cook had covered about 260 yards before Mr Armfield followed on his mare which was described as being 28 years old and blind in one eye but nevertheless was the bookies favourite at 2 to 1. Cook's hope that the mare would refuse the jumps or knock them over was not realised as she jumped beautifully and passed Cook on the second of the stipulated six laps and went on to win in nine and a half minutes.

While 'Bell's Life' carried results from a variety of sporting events throughout England it was quite amazing that side by side with them were also results from army sports held in the Crimea as that war approached its end.

On Whit Monday May 12, Bob Sadler advertised a 'Great Metropolitan Handicap' of one lap of the 580 yards circuit with prizes of £7.10.0 (£7.50), £2 and 10/- (50p). Entry could be made at Mr Wilson's 'Spotted Dog' in the Strand or at Mr Sadler's for 1/- (5p) and 1/6 (7½p) more if accepted. He also announced that any person entering under a wrong name would be disqualified and that entry was open to all the world! There were 29 entries but drizzling, incessant rain and a clash with the Wandsworth Fair, meant that on the day only about half the entries turned up and the spectator attendance was also poor. Five heats were run and at about 7.00 pm the final took place with Harry Margetts beating James Pudney by a couple of yards, both men having gone off an 18 yard start mark. If the lap of Bob Sadler's

track was only 580 yards, which was what the advertising had said, then the course was not an accurate three laps to the mile as it would fall twenty yards short.

Mr Armfield brought his mare 'Polly' back to Garratt Lane on Monday June 2 for an unusual match against two of the country's best known pedestrians. The wager for £20 a side was that his mare could beat James Pudney and William Jackson over one mile with them running half a mile each, while he would ride the mare and jump eight three foot six inch hurdles and would dismount and remount the mare after each jump. A large number of people had been attracted to view the spectacle as 'Polly' was quite a celebrity herself, having previously been a member of Monsieur Tournaire's French equestrian troupe and was extremely well trained and docile. Mr Armfield was to ride on the inside of the course with the pedestrians running on the outside and it had been calculated that because of this, he should allow the runners a 98 yards start. James Pudney and the mare took up their positions and at a flag signal both man and horse started. At the end of Pudney's half mile he had been caught and he handed over to Jackson almost abreast with the horse and rider. As Pudney had been considered the faster of the two runners and had been defeated by 98 yards, Jackson was considered to have no chance and so it proved, as despite his efforts the race finished with him coming home thirty to forty yards in the rear. The mare was timed in at 4 minutes 11 seconds and it was reported that one lucky punter had backed the mare for 100 sovereigns.

The contemporary descriptions of these races with the horse and rider performing on the track while the pedestrians ran outside ropes which were on the outside of the track would indicate that spectators would have been restricted to the inside of the arena otherwise they would have obstructed the pedestrians. This appeared to be a quite normal arrangement in these early days of enclosed arenas and before it became necessary to have the centre of the arena clear of spectators so that field events could take place in relative safety.

Another contest involving 'Polly' was arranged for Wednesday July 16. On this occasion Mr Armfield had backed his mare to run 150 yards and clear ten hurdles quicker than a pedestrian known as Oldham could run 130 yards and clear eight hurdles. The decision of the referee was a dead heat as he considered Oldham to have landed off the last hurdle at exactly the same time as Polly's back legs. To resolve the matter, they competed again with exactly the same terms on Monday July 28 and on this occasion Mr Armfield and the horse won the contest by fifteen yards.

CHAPTER 8
1856-1857
James Pudney versus John Levett for the 10 miles championship

Despite the fact that events were regularly been held at the ground, Bob Sadler had made a big decision. In *'Bell's Life'* published on Sunday August 17 there appeared the following announcement:-

'MR SADLER, of the Race Ground, Garratt Lane, Wandsworth, informs the public that the above premises will be sold, in consequence of which Mr Sadler intends, for the last race at Garratt Lane before he gives up possession, depositing the sum of £20 with the Editor of 'Bell's Life', to be given to the man who will run the greatest distance in one hour, on September 8; open to the world: all to start from scratch; each man to pay 5s (25p) entrance, which will be added to the £20 to go to the first man; the second to receive £5, the third £2. Entries to be made with Mr Sadler or at Mr Wilson's,' Spotted Dog', Strand, on or before September 2, after which day no one will be allowed to enter'.

Six days later on August 23 under a heading *'Wandsworth, Surrey, adjoining (sic) Garratt Great Green'* the sale notice for Althorp Lodge appeared in *'The Times'*. The auctioneers, Messrs Blake of Croydon, were to conduct the sale at Garraway's, Change Alley, Cornhill at noon on August 29. It was described as a substantial detached residence with planted grounds, canal, ornamental rustic bridges and buildings, a fine artesian well (forming a fountain), stabling, coach-house and convenient out buildings together with a highly productive meadow, the whole

29) GARRAWAY'S in Change Alley, Cornhill, where the auction for the sale of Althorp Lodge was held in 1856.

area comprising eight acres. Absolutely no mention whatsoever was made of the running track.

As well as the primary lot of Althorp Lodge, the ornamental gardens and the field behind which accommodated the running track, there were seven other lots in the sale. Lot two was of the ground on the southern side of Althorp Lodge and had a detached rustic cottage on the site. Lot three was a market garden area known as 'Drunken Bridge Close' which fronted on to Garratt Lane and was on the southern corner of what is now Aboyne Road. The remaining five lots were fields which comprised the area to the north of the Althorp Lodge estate up to Burntwood Lane.

The auction duly took place but no sale was achieved of the Althorp Lodge estate and Bob Sadler retained his tenure of it and all the grounds including the track. He also appears to have purchased the field comprising lot four which lay next to Althorp Lodge and fronted on to Garratt Lane.

Just three days later on Monday September 1, controversy was still plaguing the ground when for a 4 miles walking handicap between Philip Coxford from Kingsland and Joseph Jenns of Camden Town, the lateness in starting caused the *'Bell's Life'* reporter to leave the ground. The men, who had agreed in the articles to a 5.00 pm start, were unable to agree on a referee for the match and the supporters of Coxford were described as *'a set of the most ill-behaved and uncontrollable roughs imaginable'*. At dusk fell about 7.00 pm both parties agreed that Bob Sadler should act as referee and he fired the starting gun to get the race underway. Coxford had be allowed an 80 yards start but it soon became evident that maybe the advantage should have been given to Jenns who got further and further behind as Coxford came home a winner by over half a lap.

Great excitement had been engendered by Sadler's idea of a 1 Hour race which he had advertised in mid August. On Monday September 8 about a thousand arrived at the ground hoping to see a fine race between the four top pedestrians who had entered namely:- James Pudney of Mile End, William Jackson *'The American Deer'*, James Rowan of Gateshead and John Syddall of Sheffield. They were disappointed however to learn that Rowan had not travelled from the North East at all and Syddall, although at the ground, had not felt well enough to run. Their entry fee of £5 had boosted the prize money to £40 and it had been intended that £33 would go to the winner, £5 to the second and had there been a third finisher he would have received £2.

The race started at nine minutes past five o'clock and Pudney and Jackson set off at a very fast pace passing the first mile in 4:45. Still running closely together, the 5 miles mark passed in 27:11 and they were still together at 10 miles in 56:40. In the remaining 3 minutes 20 seconds they ran shoulder to shoulder and when they had reached about the middle of the third stretch on the thirty second lap, the hour was up and they had run 10 miles 955 yards. Bob Sadler was acting as referee and his decision was that the men had run a dead heat although many onlookers felt that Jackson was just leading when the hour expired. In effect, this decision would mean that the men would have to run again to resolve the prize and this caused *'Bell's Life'* to make the critical comment:-

'We cannot but express our disapproval of the conduct of Mr Sadler in acting as referee for his own money! It was to say the least unseemly and naturally excited much suspicion'.

To resolve the dead heat race of September 8, Jackson and Pudney had arranged another match at Garratt Lane but this time instead of racing for 1 hour, it was to decide who would be the fastest over 11 miles. Pudney undertook his training for the event in the vicinity of Deal while Jackson prepared in and around Wandsworth. Eight to nine hundred were attracted to the event and the prize on offer this time was said to be £40 put up by Bob Sadler. The men were ready to race at 5.30 pm and Jackson led through the first mile in 4:45 and although he continued to lead throughout the third and fourth miles, Pudney always appeared to be running easily and towards the finish of the seventh mile he moved into the lead and Jackson, who had begun to look tired and haggard, gave up the race two laps later. With the contest now over Pudney reduced his pace but carried on to complete the 11 miles in 60:45. At 35, Jackson was some nine years older than Pudney, but his failure to finish was met with both surprise and disappointment. On Monday November 17 yet another race between the two men took place at Garratt Lane this time over 10 miles for £25 a side and Pudney won with the greatest of ease in 55:30. The regulars at Mr Sadler's ground had now watched nobody but Jackson and Pudney race at the ground in the last three events held there during the autumn of 1856 and Pudney had demonstrated his complete dominance over Jackson.

Early in 1857, a new method of getting to Bob Sadler's track was mentioned in advertising the events at the facility. A railway station had just been opened at Wandsworth Common and although it would involve a longish walk down Burntwood Lane it was no further away than the other stations that served the track at Wimbledon and Wandsworth Town. The line through Wandsworth Common then connected with the main London terminus of London Bridge.

The first match of the year was on January 12 and involved a man George Martin, who would in a few years time play a very prominent part in the history of the track. On this fine but cold evening he was engaged in a 130 yards race with John Smith *'The Regent Street Pet'* who would receive a five yard start. In the course of the distance, they would have to jump five 3 feet 2 inch hurdles placed equidistant apart, with the winner being the man who landed off the final hurdle first. The start was by mutual agreement and following five false starts they eventually got underway and only losing a couple of yards from his five yards advantage, Smith came in the winner by two yards.

The following afternoon Philip Coxford and John Hotine met in a 7 miles walking match but before they had even completed two laps they had both broken into an unmistakable trot. Immediately the appointed referee disqualified both men, declared the match off and left the ground. The match was rearranged for Tuesday February 10 but because of England's boxing champion Tom Sayers fight against Aaron Jones which would take away potential spectators, it was decided to have a further postponement until the following Wednesday February 18. It was a titanic battle over 21 laps with the lead changing frequently and the excitement amongst the onlookers was at fever pitch as they began the final lap still locked together, with only seventy yards remaining Coxford gave in and Hotine came into the finish to win in 56:29.

More trouble had come for Bob Sadler at the end of January. A match of one and a half miles for £15 a side between George Chick of Walworth and William Priestley of Bermondsey, in which Sadler acted as the referee, was abandoned when he ruled foul play on both sides following a collision between the two men. In another match on the same evening over 140 yards, between Edwin Reed of Bermondsey and James Stainer of Marylebone for £5 a side, because of the delay in starting caused by the pedestrians, the chosen referee resigned his office as he considered it too dark for him to decide the result in the event of a close finish.

At the end of March on a day of continuous heavy rain, three to four hundred assembled to watch a 7 miles walking match between Joseph Plumbton of Westminster and David Broad of Fulham. It was due to start between 3 and 4 o'clock but due to the pedestrians and their backers not being able to agree on a referee, it was well past 5 o'clock when Bob Sadler was eventually appointed to act in that capacity. The late arrival of competitors and the delays caused by the 'mutual start' method of starting races came in for repeated complaints.

30) Right: The sale notice for Althorp Lodge and various surrounding land that appeared in 'The Times' on August 23 1856.

31) Below: The plan of the freehold estate offered for sale. The square shaped running track is clearly defined in Lot 1 although no mention is made of it in the description of the lots which follow on the next two pages (Illustrations 32/33). (All courtesy of Wandsworth Heritage Service).

Wandsworth, Surrey, adjoining Garrett Great-green.

MESSRS. BLAKE will SELL by AUCTION, at Garraway's, on Friday, August 29, at 12, a compact and valuable FREEHOLD ESTATE, known as Althorp Lodge, with possession, eligibly situate on the high road from Wandsworth to Tooting, and opposite the road leading to the Wimbledon Railway Station (which is distant about two miles); comprising a substantial detached residence, with planted grounds, canal, ornamental rustic bridges and buildings, a fine artesian well (forming a fountain), stabling, coach-house, and convenient out-buildings, together with a highly productive meadow, the whole comprising an area of eight acres, now in the occupation of Mr. Robert Sadler, whose tenancy will terminate on the completion of the purchase; also a small rustic cottage, with garden and orchard, five plots of building land, having capital frontages of 1,200 feet, and comprising an area of eight acres, now in garden cultivation, and a detached corner plot of land, containing about 1¼ acre, nearly opposite St. Clement Danes Alms-houses. Particulars may be had (14 days before the sale) upon the premises; at the inns in the neighbourhood; at Garraway's; the Artichoke Inn, Newington-causeway; of Messrs. Chester and Son, solicitors, Church-row, Newington-butts; and of Messrs. Blake, Croydon.

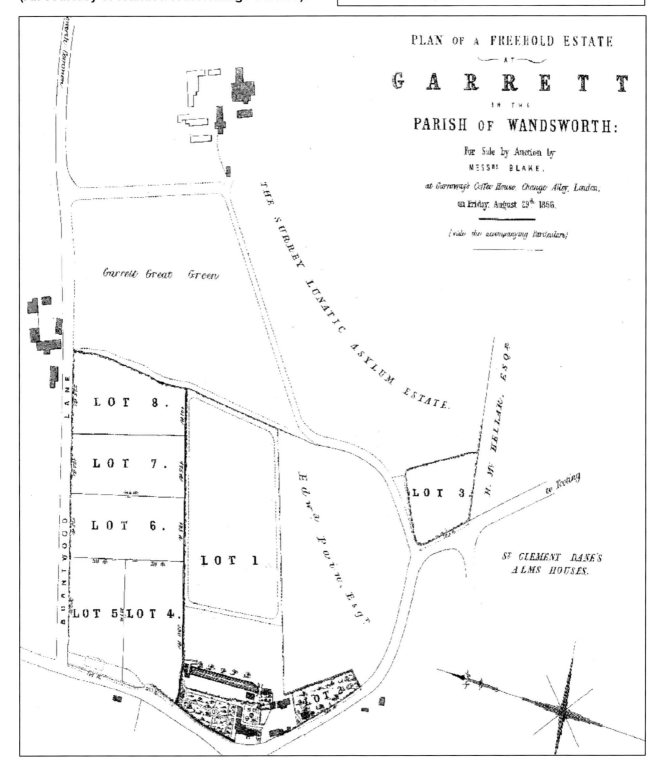

PLAN OF A FREEHOLD ESTATE

AT

G A R R E T T

IN THE

PARISH OF WANDSWORTH:

For Sale by Auction by

MESSRS BLAKE,

at Garraway's Coffee House, Change Alley, London,

on Friday, August 29th 1856.

[vide the accompanying Particulars]

THE SURREY LUNATIC ASYLUM ESTATE.

Garrett Great Green

LOT 8.

LOT 7.

LOT 6.

LOT 1

LOT 5 LOT 4.

LOT 3

H. Mr. HELLIC. ESQR.

to Tooting

Edwa Pow. Esqr

St CLEMENT DANES ALMS HOUSES.

BURNTWOOD LANE

GARRETT, IN THE PARISH OF WANDSWORTH,

SURREY,

About 1½ Mile from the WANDSWORTH STATION, and 1½ Mile from the WIMBLEDON STATION.

Particulars and Conditions of Sale.

LOT 1.

(COLOURED GREEN UPON THE PLAN ANNEXED.)

A COMPACT & VALUABLE FREEHOLD ESTATE,

KNOWN AS "ALTHORP LODGE,"

(WITH POSSESSION,)

Eligibly situate on the High Road from WANDSWORTH to TOOTING, and opposite the Road leading to the WIMBLEDON RAILWAY STATION;

COMPRISING

A Substantial Detached Residence,

PRINCIPALLY BRICK BUILT, WITH ORNAMENTAL COMPOSITION EXTERIOR, PORTICO ENTRANCE TO FRONT, AND VERANDA AT BACK;—CONTAINING

On the Two Pair—3 Chambers. On the One Pair—3 Bed Rooms, Dressing Room, large Room with low Ceiling, and Water Closet. On the Ground Floor an Entrance Lobby with Iron Balustrades, and mahogany Hand Rail to Staircase, Sitting Room, with gothic-marble Chimney Piece, and French Ornaments opening to a Greenhouse, a similar Room with marble Chimney Piece, (now used as an open Bar,) a smaller Room communicating, with Scullery adjoining, and stone-paved Kitchen;—a timber and slated Building adjoining, consisting of a second Kitchen, Brewhouse, Dairy, with slate shelves and galley-tile linings.

A DETACHED SUMMER OR BILLIARD ROOM,

With Marble Chimney Piece, Ornamented French Casements, and Sash Door;

LAWN, PLANTED WITH WALNUT TREES & SHRUBS;

PRODUCTIVE GARDEN, STOCKED WITH FRUIT TREES;

MELON GROUND, WITH FORCING PIT AND LIGHTS;

BOWLING GREEN & CANAL;

WITH A

FINE ARTESIAN WELL, WHICH FORMS A FOUNTAIN,

AND SUPPLIES ANOTHER FOUNTAIN IN THE GARDEN;

EXPENSIVELY-FORMED & ORNAMENTAL RUSTIC BRIDGES & BUILDINGS;

A COMMODIOUS YARD,

With 3-STALL STABLE, COACH HOUSE, LOOSE BOX with LOFT over, a Lean-to COW HOUSE with Calf Pen, A DOUBLE-BAYED BARN with THRASHING FLOOR, CART HOUSE, &c.—together with

A HIGHLY PRODUCTIVE MEADOW;

The whole comprising an Area of 7a. 2r. 26p.,

(OR THE SAME MORE OR LESS.)

LOT 2.

(COLOURED BUFF UPON THE PLAN ANNEXED.)

A FREEHOLD ESTATE,

(WITH POSSESSION;)

COMPRISING

A DETACHED RUSTIC COTTAGE,

THE EXTERIOR EXPENSIVELY FORMED OF POTTERY CLINKERS, WITH ORNAMENTAL TILE ROOF;

Containing three Rooms, with a lean-to Porch, Garden, and Orchard; having a Frontage of about 204-ft. to the HIGH ROAD, and containing 0A. 1R. 35P. (be the same more or less.)

LOT 3.

(COLOURED PINK UPON THE PLAN ANNEXED.)

A CORNER PLOT OF VALUABLE FREEHOLD BUILDING LAND,

CALLED "DRUNKEN BRIDGE CLOSE,"

NOW USED FOR MARKET GARDEN PURPOSES,

Containing 1A. 0R. 14P., (be the same more or less;) having a capital Frontage of about 205-ft. to the HIGH ROAD leading to Tooting, and lying nearly opposite St. Clement Danes Alms' Houses.

THE FIVE FOLLOWING LOTS (which are coloured Blue upon the accompanying Plan) comprise an Area of 8A. 1R. 14P., (be the same more or less,) and consist of

A VALUABLE CLOSE OF MARKET GARDEN LAND,

Adjoining Lot 1, and known as "Garrett's Close," otherwise "Burnt Wood Lane Field," including a small portion of "Moor Close," adjoining on the South, and Land formerly belonging to the "Surrey Iron Railway Company" adjoining partly on the West.

LOT 4.

A Valuable Plot of Freehold Building Land,

Having a Frontage of 208-ft. to the HIGH ROAD from WANDSWORTH to TOOTING, by a mean Depth of about 363-ft., and containing 1A. 3R. 1P. (be the same more or less.)

LOT 5.

A Highly-Valuable Corner Plot of Freehold Building Land,

Having Frontages of 507-ft. to the HIGH ROAD from WANDSWORTH to TOOTING and to BURNT WOOD LANE, and containing 1A. 1R. 39P. (be the same more or less.)

LOT 6.

A Valuable Plot of Freehold Building Land,

Having a Frontage of 175-ft. to BURNT WOOD LANE, by a mean Depth of about 414-ft., and containing 1A. 2R. 27P. (be the same more or less.)

LOT 7.

A Valuable Plot of Freehold Building Land,

Having a Frontage of 175-ft. to BURNT WOOD LANE, by a mean Depth of about 414-ft., and containing 1A. 2R. 27P. (be the same more or less.)

LOT 8.

A Valuable Plot of Freehold Building Land,

Having a Frontage of 225-ft. to BURNT WOOD LANE, by a Depth of about 414-ft., and containing 1A. 3R. 0P. (be the same more or less.)

The Vendor reserves the right of offering the last-mentioned five Lots in one Lot, if he should so determine at the time of Sale.

The Purchasers are to make and maintain good and sufficient Fences on such sides of their Lots as are denoted by the mark T within the Lots upon the accompanying Plan.

The whole of the Property included in this sale is in the occupation of Mr. ROBERT SADLER, whose Tenancy will terminate on the completion of the respective Purchases; at which time the Purchaser of Lot 1 shall take, at a fair Valuation to be previously made in the usual way, such Tenant's Fixtures, fixed Bar and Trade Fittings, as belong to the said ROBERT SADLER, and which will be set forth in an Inventory to be produced at the time of Sale; and the Purchasers of the remaining Lots shall take, in like manner, such Crops as may be growing upon the Arable Lands, and any Labour and Dressings upon the aforecropped Land which may be prepared for a future Crop; and the amount of the respective Valuations shall be paid on the completion of the respective Purchases.

Such Fixtures in Lot 1 as belong to the Vendor, and the Growing Timber or other Trees upon each Lot, will be included in the Purchase.

☞ Particulars with Plans may be had upon the Premises; at the Spread Eagle, Wandsworth; Raven, Battersea; Dog & Fox, Wimbledon; Bell's, Putney; Plough, Clapham; Castle, Tooting; King's Head, Mitcham; Bell, Merton; at Garraway's Coffee House; the Artichoke Inn, Newington Causeway; of Messrs. Cruttwell and Son, Solicitors, Clark Row, Newington Butts, of Messrs. Robinson and TEMPLE, Salle-fore, 48, Conduit Street, Hanover Square; and of Messrs. BLAKE, Croydon.

34) A modern view from Garratt Green, looking towards Garratt Lane, to where the running track once stood but which is now covered with a housing estate.

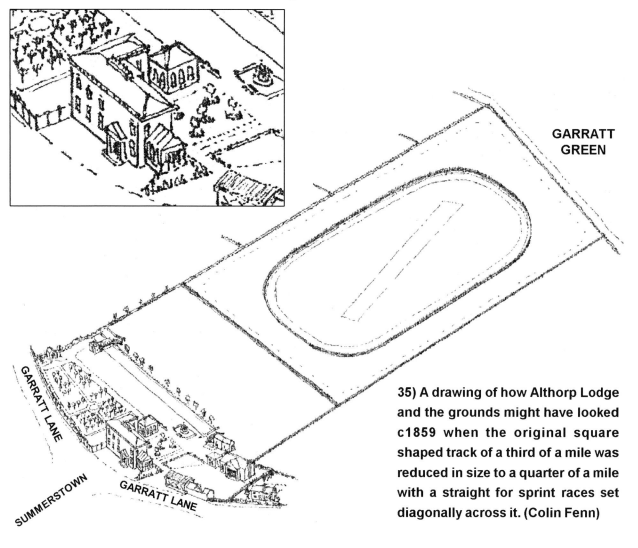

GARRATT GREEN

GARRATT LANE

SUMMERSTOWN

GARRATT LANE

35) A drawing of how Althorp Lodge and the grounds might have looked c1859 when the original square shaped track of a third of a mile was reduced in size to a quarter of a mile with a straight for sprint races set diagonally across it. (Colin Fenn)

Bob Sadler was putting together an Easter programme to entice numbers to the track. On Good Friday April 10 he put up three prizes of £5, £1 and 10/- (50p) and arranged an open handicap race over one lap of the track, advertised as 580 yards and the entries he attracted meant four qualifying rounds were necessary. On the same day a novice Richard Spice backed himself against time in trying to walk six and a half miles within an hour. Sad to relate that he failed when having taken fifty eight minutes to walk six miles he did not finish the final half mile. There was also a 6 mile walking contest between Joseph Clarke and 'The Darkie'. Clarke gave up what had been a close contest after the fourth mile and 'The Darkie' is recorded as having then put on his coat and completed the eighteen laps for victory. On Easter Monday, several hundred witnessed a fine race over two laps of the course (1160 yards), in a challenge between Charles Cook of Marylebone and Richard Eden of Barnes for £5 a side. A sudden shower of hail just before the start did not deter the men and Cook came home in a thrilling finish to beat Eden by less than a yard. This was followed by a 1 mile handicap won by Jeremiah Mahoney from Cook.

A good crowd attended the ground for the next holiday date of Whitsun a few weeks later on June 1 and a 10 miles handicap with prizes totalling £15 attracted some big names including James Pudney but the victory was carried off by a virtually unknown pedestrian called Dixon as the bigger names failed to close up the 6 minute lead he had been awarded by handicapper Bill Price. Bob Sadler had put up a silver snuff-box as the prize for a 2 miles event and a 150 yards handicap match completed the programme.

For some time a 10 miles match between two celebrated pedestrians James Pudney and John Levett had been mooted. The match had failed to come off In mid March when Levett had injured himself and had to forfeit £45 to Pudney. It was then intended that the match should take place on Good Friday but this also failed to materialise. Although a Battersea man, Levett had moved to Scotland and had carried out much of his training at Musselburgh Race Course near Edinburgh. The stakes were £50 from Pudney against £40 from Levett and had been lodged with the stake holders 'Bell's Life'. The event was now arranged to take place at Garratt Lane on June 10 and was advertised as a race for the 10 miles championship with the stakes and the Champions Belt to go to the victor. They had raced each other previously on many occasions. On March 6 1854 they had competed with several others at Sheffield for the 10 miles Champion's Belt with Pudney coming home about a hundred yards ahead of Levett. A return was arranged in Sheffield on June 5, when Levett suffering from stomach cramp was forced to retire at 7 miles with Pudney going on to win in 54:15.

They had also met on three previous occasions at Garratt Lane in the spring of 1855 with Levett off 200 yards winning a 10 miles handicap, Pudney winning a 6 miles handicap and both of them losing to Cook in another 10 miles handicap but with Putney finishing ahead of Levett in second place. Now at last this race would decide if Pudney was a worthy champion and with remarkably fine weather on the day, a huge crowd numbering some 3000 assembled at the Garratt Lane ground and included the expected professional supporters of pedestrianism as well as many aristocratic amateurs. Bob Sadler received acclaim for the course being in fine condition and for his efforts in making sure that all matters were carried out in a fair, respectable and honourable manner. With the betting at 6 to 4 on Pudney, the men made their appearance at 5.30 pm and about a quarter of an hour later, were ready on the scratch mark. For the first couple of miles they ran closely together but in the third mile Pudney opened a gap which he increased so that by the end of the fourth mile he led by some 140 yards passing in 20:45 and through the half way mark in 25:55 when the odds had increased to 20 to 1 on him. Levett gave up the struggle at the end of his sixth mile and Pudney completed the distance untroubled in 58:18 to claim the £90 stake and retain his champion's belt.

Events continued at the ground on virtually a weekly basis and on July 20 the first recorded field event took place there. It was a match for £10 a side between William Jackson of London and Jeremiah Mahoney from Bermondsey where each man would perform five standing jumps with the best total distance to take the £20 prize. Mahoney was allowed one foot advantage and the rules were that each man would be allowed four attempts with a five minute recovery between each effort. Although the weather on the evening was fine, the event was sparsely attended, being confined to the backers, immediate friends of the two men, the umpires and the appointed referee Bill Price. The men carried balancing weights in each hand and on the first attempt, Jackson jumped sixteen inches further but Mahoney improved on this by six inches in his second trial. Jackson's third attempt saw him again take the lead by thirty inches which Mahoney was unable to better and lost the contest by two feet despite his initial handicap advantage. The total distance achieved by Jackson was nineteen yards one foot four inches with an average of eleven feet eight inches for each attempt.

The same Jeremiah Mahoney was involved in an extraordinary incident at the track a couple of weeks later when as he approached the finish to win a heat of a 440 yards race, he was struck by a kick aimed at him from one of the spectators. The culprit was apprehended by the police and proved to be the brother of his opponent.

As previously mentioned, there were numerous occasions when pedestrians would not appear at the track until well after the appointed start time, this lackadaisical approach plus the 'mutual consent' method of starting races continued to cause huge delays at many of the events and always came in for massive criticism in the pages of 'Bell's Life'. It appears that a competitor could hold up an event by refusing to race unless they felt the start had been of some advantage to them. Sometimes two competitors would make dozens of attempts before they would both go off and could be together on the start line for well over an hour. For spectators this must have been very tedious and annoying as they could never know when an event would actually start, also, other events to follow would be delayed and sometimes have to be cancelled because of failing light. On many occasions, the referee and newspaper reporters would leave the ground in total frustration. Another cause for delays was when a referee had not been appointed in advance and it was left to be decided from those present at the event. Other methods of starting races such as the 'drop of a hat' or the 'pull of a handkerchief' were tried but it was not until the 'report of a pistol' became the normal method of starting and officials appointed well in advance, that these annoying aspects of the sport would disappear. Apart from delays, even worse was when a crowd had assembled, newspaper reporters had made the journey down to Garratt Lane and the pedestrians failed to make any appearance at all. One such occasion was on Monday August 31 1857 when two Battersea men, Thomas Harvey and Samuel Mills had arranged a 150 yards match for £5 a side. In their issue of September 9, 'Bell's Life' was not happy:-

'We had been given to understand that these men were to have run 150 yards for £5 a side on Monday last at Garratt Lane, Wandsworth but on our reporter arriving there, to his great annoyance and disappointment, he found that neither party were forthcoming. This system of stating to us that such and such a race is to come off at a certain time and place, occasioning us thereby to give it publicity in our columns and the parties subsequently failing to carry out the arrangements, is highly reprehensible and shall be discontinued by us as far as in our power lies. It is misleading us, disappointing the public and reflecting very little credit indeed on the parties concerned. We do all we can to prevent the insertion of any but bona fide matches'.

Also in September 1857, pedestrians George Martin and James Pudney staked £1 a side with Mr Wilson of 'The Spotted Dog', Strand for Martin to find a man to race Pudney over 2 miles at the Wandsworth track for £50 a side with Pudney to give £5 and share the gate money and for the editor of 'Bell's Life' to be the stakeholder. The man Martin found was John Trainer of Liverpool and the event was arranged for

November 16 and was expected to attract a huge crowd to Garratt Lane. This match would have been one of George Martin's early moves in his change from an active pedestrian to promoter, a move that would eventually have a huge impact on the sport of pedestrianism.

A very curious race happened on the track on October 5 when a 1 mile match between Mr Fox and Mr Lovett was arranged. It would be for £5 a side and the stakes were to be held by Charles Westhall. The point of curiosity was that both men each had a wooden leg. A large number of their friends were in attendance and quite a few others were attracted by the strangeness of the match. At 4.00 pm the monopedists were sent on their way having to cover three laps of the track. Fox was the early leader but only for half a lap when Lovett took over and gradually increased his lead to come in an easy winner by 100 yards in 11:34.

A good insight into the conduction of a pedestrian event is provided with the report of the match between George Brown of Hungerford Market and Joseph Jenns of Camden Town who contested a 7 miles walk at Garratt Lane on October 28. At the start the men were questioned with 'Are you both ready?' before the gun was fired which compares with the modern instruction of 'On your marks' given today. William Newman and Billy Bushy were the attendants for the competitors and a referee was appointed who decided that the best way to observe matters was to follow behind the athletes and warn them if they were infringing the walking rules by shouting 'heel down'. The spectacle therefore was of five men navigating the track while only two of them were actually in competition.

As the year drew to a close there were two events at Garratt Lane deserving of mention. Firstly the great 6 miles match between James Pudney and John Trainer on November 16 and secondly the Indian Relief Fund event held there the following week. This was the year of the Indian Mutiny and other sports meetings had also held benefit events to aid those who had suffered. The pedestrian community wanted to do something and firstly attempted to hold a grand pedestrian event at Lord's Cricket Ground. Perhaps because of the rowdy crowds that often followed pedestrianism, Mr Dark, who managed Lord's, refused permission for its use and the event was then arranged to be held at Bob Sadler's ground.

The long awaited 2 miles match between Pudney and Trainer attracted a huge crowd. It was a match for £100 staked and Pudney had also paid £5 to cover Trainer's travelling expenses. Trainer had gained his prominence in events at Liverpool and Manchester while Pudney's reputation had mostly been gained in his native London. He had competed many times at the Garratt Lane track and probably had become a bit of a local favourite. The weather, considering it was the middle of November, was remarkably fine and the referee was a man from the *'Bell's Life'* office. The men stood at the scratch line just after the appointed time of 3.00 pm but still spent about ten minutes dodging around before they actually managed to start. Trainer was the early leader but after a couple of laps Pudney took over and at the beginning of the fifth lap increased the pace to open up a 20 yards lead and despite the fact that only one further lap remained, Trainer chose not to finish the distance and Pudney ran on to complete the sixth lap for an easy victory. It was arranged that Pudney, who was the proprietor of the *'Coach and Horses'* in Back Church Lane, Commercial Road, would receive the £100 stake at his own premises on the following Thursday. It did not appear that Trainer had done anything else other than failing to finish yet he issued a statement saying that he would not be able to undertake any further races in the near future as he had seriously injured himself.

The India Relief event on November 23 took the form of three races, a lap of the track of 580 yards, a 4 miles walk and a 3 miles race. Some very prominent pedestrians gave their services for no payment or prizes and the gate money would be given to the fund. The day arrived but the weather was so bad and the attendance so poor that it was decided to postpone the event until New Year's Day 1858 but for some reason it does not appear to have actually ever taken place.

The final event to conclude Bob Sadler's fifth year of operation at Garratt Lane took place on Boxing Day when one of the events contested was a 100 yards match between Lt Col John Astley of the Scots Fusilier Guards and Captain Smith of the 71st Highlands. Neither man earned his living as a professional runner but were gentleman amateurs prepared to wage £25 each on their ability. Astley, born in 1828, was the second son of the second baronet Sir Dugdale Astley and had attended Eton and Christ Church Oxford before enlisting in the army at the age of 20. He was initially stationed in Ireland before his regiment was transferred to the Crimea where he was invalided home following the battle of the Alma. He had a huge interest in sport generally, including Hunting, Coursing, Running, Rowing, Cricket, Boxing, Football and even Whippet Racing. He became a prominent race horse owner, had laid out the Hamilton Park racecourse and formed the Hurst Park Syndicate to convert the old Hampton course into an enclosed meeting. At one time he owned the Orleans Club at Twickenham, at another he was Chairman of the Pelican Club and subsequently President of The Sports Club. He was a staunch supporter of Boxing, rarely missing an event at the National Sporting Club and he subsequently became a promoter of long distance indoor pedestrian races at the Agricultural Hall in Islington where the coveted Astley Belt would be contested. A huge name in Victorian sporting circles, he became known as 'The Mate' and it was this winning performance by a good yard over

36) All round sportsman SIR JOHN ASTLEY (1828-1894) who ran his last ever race at the Garratt Lane ground on Boxing Day 1857. He later became well known for his promotion of six day races at the Agricultural Hall, Islington, which is currently the Business Design Centre.

Captain Smith at the Garratt Lane track that proved to be his last outing as a competitive athlete. Before leaving Garratt Lane that day, he ran a quarter of a mile uncontested and recorded a useful 54 seconds.

In Astley's biography published in 1894 just prior to his death, he said it was the first and only time that his father had ever been present at one of his matches and that two or three of his brothers were also in attendance at Garratt Lane that day.

CHAPTER 9

1858

William Spooner against Charles Westhall in a 20 miles walk

The first big match of the new year 1858 was a 20 miles handicap walk between two of the country's most famous pedestrians, William Spooner who had been trained by the man who was to become his father in law, John Smith the *'Regent Street Pet'*, who operated from his public house *'The Vale Arms'* at Hammersmith Gate and the renowned Charles Westhall. Special transport was even laid on to bring more of Westhall's supporters from *'The Derby Arms'* at Turnham Green. The umpires and referee having been agreed on, they took up their position on an elevated position in the centre of the ground. Spooner who was many years the junior of Westhall, had allowed him a two minute start. Despite the very raw and wintery weather, a large number were attracted to the ground to watch these top men in action. As Spooner set off, Westhall's handicap allowance had enabled him to gain about a 510 yard lead.. By the end of the seventh mile, Westhall had even increased this lead but from that point onwards Spooner began to cut back his advantage and by the half distance Westhall's lead had been reduced to about 380 yards and by the start of the fourteenth mile was only 60 yards in arrears. As they started out on the fifteenth mile, Spooner hit the front and Westhall soon afterwards gave up the chase. There was some dispute about the fairness of Spooner's walking and the umpires and referee were requested to attend *'Bell's Life'* to make a final adjudication on the result. The findings of this inquest were that the result should stand as the appointed referee, a Mr Jones, had not received any appeal on the day. *'Bell's Life'* did however state that they felt walking matches of importance should take place in the open and not on enclosed grounds where no order is kept and the men's legs could not always be seen by the officials. Nowadays, it would be more likely that the opposite would apply.

37) Prominent long distance walker WILLIAM SPOONER (1832-?) (right) with his trainer and father in law JOHN SMITH 'The Regent Street pet' (1819-1892), who himself was an outstanding sprinter and hurdler. At various times he was proprietor of *'The Vale Arms'* at Hammersmith, *'The Normand Arms'* in Fulham and *'The Prince of Wales Tavern'* in Turnham Green.

Another good crowd were attracted to the ground the following week when Thomas Cummings a native of Portsmouth but now based in London and Job Smith, one of the top northern pedestrians from Manchester, contested a 6 miles race for £30 a side with Cummings having paid £5 towards Smith's travelling expenses and with the agreement that both men would share the gate money. To achieve an exact six miles, the pedestrians would have to complete eighteen laps of the 580 yards track with an additional further 120 yards. It was a keenly contested race with Cummings leading for most of the distance but quite often the men running shoulder to shoulder. The race took a dramatic turn when on the seventeenth lap Smith reeling from sheer exhaustion, fell against the rails surrounding the course and Cummings completed the course in a very commendable 32:00 although the very exactness of this reported time leads to some doubt about its correctness.

An interesting event took place on February 15 when Oliver Forster of the Haymarket and George Brown of Hungerford Market contested a 2 miles race with the first mile to be walked and the second to be run. Although Brown was leading at the end of the walk, Forster pegged him back during the run and came home the winner by just two yards in 18:30.

A return match was arranged between Thomas Cummings and Job Smith for March 15 over 2 miles and Job Smith made another trip down to London receiving £3 from Cummings for his consent in letting the race be run in London. Just after the appointed 3.00 pm start time the men made their appearance. The appointed starter asked them *'Are you ready'* and then fired the gun. Cummings went straight to the front at a tremendous pace but was closely followed by Smith. It remained this way until Smith made his challenge with a lap and a half remaining and after taking the lead, gradually increased it to twenty yards by the finish in a fine 9:51. Job Smith had gained revenge for his January defeat and he was destined to make another very dramatic appearance at Garratt Lane but not for another four years.

Bob Sadler was arranging two handicap races on Good Friday April 2. A 580 yards race over one lap of the track with four heats and a final and another over 2 miles. In an effort to improve on the conduct of the meeting, the advertising stated that any party not being on the mark two minutes before starting will be disqualified also anyone making a false start before the gun is fired would be put back three yards. He was definitely trying to improve the reputation of the ground when on June 3 he did not allow any gate money to be taken for a 200 yard handicap between Young Tyrell of Stepney and Thomas Brown of Bethnal Green because. Sadler obviously doubted the validity of the match and the fact that there was no responsible stakeholder and he went as far as to state that he would not allow any match on his ground in the future unless he had a guarantee as to a match being of a bona fide character, or *'Bell's Life'* being the stakeholder.

There was a very unusual event held on Wednesday May 12. William Payne of Croydon had wagered the sum of £25 against Time that he and his three brothers, Richard, Charles and Joseph, should aggregately walk 24 miles in 4 hours. Each brother would be allowed to walk for an hour and therefore had to average 6 miles each to win the wager. Despite heavy rain falling, a large crowd attended and forty to fifty carriages and other vehicles were packed into the courtyard attached to Althorp Lodge. Mr Clements,

previously proprietor of *'The Angel'*, Croydon, was appointed umpire for the Payne's and Mr Edward Atteridge of *'The Queen's Head'*, Beddington Corner, was appointed timekeeper while the famous pedestrian Charles Westhall was chosen as referee. For the four hour journey, the umpires had decided to follow the walkers around the track in a Dog Cart. The event started with the diminutive 5 feet 5 ½ inch William just after 2.00 pm and at the end of his allotted hour, had walked 5 miles 1240 yards. The next brother to walk was Richard and he added 6 miles 823 yards to the total. It was then the turn of Charles and his total of 6 miles 1061 yards left the last brother Joseph a relatively easy task and he came over the 24 miles mark in 3 hours 49 minutes 10 seconds, so winning the wager by 10 minutes 50 seconds. Their combined efforts would no doubt have left them somewhat thirsty but there is no record of how much of their winnings were spent at Bob Sadler's *'Wellington Inn'* before the four brothers made their way home to Croydon.

On Whit Monday May 24 Sadler repeated his Easter programme idea of a 1 lap handicap event and he offered three prizes of £7, a silver watch, and 10/- (50p). There would also be a 4 miles handicap walk with three prizes of a silver watch, 10/- (50p) and 5/- (25p) and a 300 yards novices race for those who had never won more than £1 and again providing the three prizes of a silver watch, 5/- (25p) and half a crown (12½p). Unfavourable weather prevented them taking place and they were rescheduled for June 21.

A match on June 7 between James Stainer of St John's Wood and Jerry Cromey of Marylebone caused *'Bell's Life'* to comment:-

38) A dog cart was used by the officials to follow the unusual event held on the track on May 12 1858 when four brothers from Croydon successfully wagered that by walking for an hour each they would complete a total of twenty four miles within four hours.

'The attendance as regards quantity was of a fair average amount but in quality was one of the most ill-behaved and actually ferocious that we have ever had the misfortune to meet. The 'bludgeoneers' on both sides brandished their formidable weapons to the evident intimidation of the respectable portion of the assemblage, who as a matter of course would not bet a shilling on the result. We must here throw out a suggestion to Mr Sadler, that if he wishes for the attendance of peaceable and respectable people on his grounds, he should desire his gatekeeper not to admit persons with sticks, or what an Irishman would call 'wattles' as thick as bed-posts'.

The start was to be made by the much criticised method of mutual consent and it caused the usual problems. There were about thirty five false attempts which wasted two hours forty minutes. *'Bell's Life'* was at a loss to understand why a gun start could not be employed. For a matter of record, Stainer won the race by about a yard.

The various events held at Garratt Lane never got near approaching the large number of entries achieved at other grounds such as Hyde Park in Sheffield, the Copenhagen Grounds near Manchester, the Albion Grounds in Wolverhampton, and the Salford Borough Gardens. There were also many venues in and around London catering for the sport but now a new one known as The Metropolitan Grounds, Hackney Wick began to grab the headlines. In June 1858 'Bell's Life' wrote:-

'The newly established running grounds in this locality have now acquired a celebrity that threatens to put all suburban places of a similar nature in the shade and we must say deservedly so, for the liberality of the proprietor, Mr Baum and the facility of access afforded by the railway which lands a person within a

39) The diminutive SAM BARKER 'The Billingsgate Boy' (1833-?) who was trained by Bill Price and was briefly holder of the 10 miles cup.

few yards of the scene of action, are recommendations not to be met with, we regret to say, elsewhere'.

Perhaps these comments were particularly aimed at the Garratt Lane facility.

Their report of the meeting held at Garratt Lane on Monday June 21, when the handicap races for prizes offered by Bob Sadler postponed from Whit Monday were held, does give a good description of the Garratt Lane setting despite its inaccessibility.

They reported that:-

'The day was exceedingly sultry and the roads nearly three inches deep in dust but that the country all around looked beautiful. Nature had everywhere arrayed herself in her loveliest and most enchanting garb and the harvest we presume will be an unprecedentedly abundant one, for the crops on all sides appeared in the most flourishing condition'.

Having given this glowing description of the scene, they then issued the common complaint that although the events were advertised to start at 3.00 pm it was 5.00 pm before they got underway. The next Monday they were even more incensed when a 100 yards match between Guss and Lewis, which had the 'mutual start' arrangement, was delayed by 73 false starts and they described this method of starting races as 'reprehensible'. They eventually started at 7.00 pm by the pull of a handkerchief. *'The Era'* newspaper even said that the whole affair savoured of arrangement between the two men from Clerkenwell. Another event that evening was for William Newman to walk 4 miles and then run 5 within one hour. He completed the walk in 32:10 but Charles Westhall's watch told that as he finished the 5 miles run he had failed in his task by five seconds. Philip Coxford and Joseph Jenns were then matched to walk 5 miles but the delay in the Guss v Lewis match meant that this could not take place due to darkness. The pedestrians themselves must have been as equally annoyed as the crowd and rearranged their match for the Hackney Wick ground instead of at Garratt Lane.

A future 10 miles champion competed at Garratt Lane on Wednesday August 18 when Sam Barker, who was to become known as 'The Billingsgate Boy' contested a 1 mile race with William Newey of Walworth and ran out an easy winner in just under five minutes.

Various matches continued on a regular basis but the next event that gained national prominence was a 50 miles walk between William Spooner of London and William Laycock of Bradford. Laycock initially wanted the distance to be 20 miles with him being allowed a fifteen minute start but Spooner would not agree to this and finally the 50 miles distance was agreed upon with Laycock receiving the fifteen minutes. The match was for £25 a side with Spooner contributing a further £3 for Laycock's expenses. Spooner would be attended on by John Smith while Laycock's brother would attend to his needs with James Parish of the Strand acting as referee. This was going to involve the walkers completing 150 laps of the track and the event got underway at 9.00 am on Monday October 4. During his fifteen minute allowance, Laycock covered 1 mile 1400 yards before Spooner set out in pursuit. When Spooner had completed five miles he had reduced Laycock's lead by 500 yards and continued to gain so that by twelve miles had reduced the lead by 700 yards and on the first lap of the twentieth mile he overtook Laycock and went into the lead. They then walked closely together exchanging the lead for the next three miles before Spooner made a determined effort to get away and after five hours he had covered 30 miles two laps and 100 yards and by this time had a two and a half lap lead over Laycock. Ten miles later he had increased his lead to 1 mile and two laps. At the finish of his fiftieth mile Spooner was an easy winner and the timekeeper declared his winning performance as 8 hours 27 minutes having defeated Laycock by 2 miles and 300 yards despite his quarter of an hour start advantage. Although defeated, Laycock received much praise for his gutsy performance

A large crowd was attracted to the ground a couple of weeks later to witness, amongst various other races, a very peculiar event. Two men from Chelsea, George Lovett, who was described as 'the champion of wooden legged men' and John Clifton who had deformed feet which were turned inwards, were to race over 1 mile and for them to cover the three laps necessary in 'the best way they could'. Both men were backed from 'The Stanley Tavern' in King's Road, Chelsea for a stake of £5 a side which would be held by 'Bell's Life'. As they started out the odds were 2 to 1 on Clifton and by the end of the first lap he had gained a considerable lead. Lovett stumped along behind but could make no impact on Clifton and was dead beat at three quarters of a mile which allowed Clifton to score any easy victory by over 100 yards. It was the same margin of victory for Clifton, who described himself as 'the bumble footed man' when they renewed their rivalry over 5 miles at Garratt Lane just after Christmas.

The 'mutual start' caused continual problems and delays. A match over 120 yards between George Tait and John Cook on November 1 had between thirty and forty attempts before it got underway. Quite often a start by the report of a pistol was included into the articles of agreement and an alternative of 'the first pull of a handkerchief' was sometimes the agreement but exactly how this operated is not quite clear.

There were also agreements that the course, or part of the course, for sprint races should be roped and staked. This meant that stakes would be driven into the track at intervals and joined up together with ropes so that the pedestrians would be restricted to their section of the track and be unable to cross in front of each other. Disagreements sometimes arose if this had not been done. The day after the Tait and Cook match, a 150 yards race between George Burton and William Preston caused argument because the roping and staking had not been done and the daylight was nearly gone before it could be done and the race started. The roping and staking method of restricting athletes to a lane on the track persisted for many more years and was still in evidence on some tracks even after World War two until lines marked on the track in whitewash and subsequent all weather surfaces with clearly marked lines became the standard method.

The rough element who often supported the events, were also a great cause for concern. On November 8, in a 10 miles walking match between Richard Owen and Joseph Walton, both from Lambeth, Walton won the event by 150 yards but 'Bell's Life' reported:-

'The Lambeth costermongers; we are informed, behaved in a very unmanly manner, and threatened the winner with their vengeance'.

The unruly crowd often fuelled by alcohol and of course anxious to support their man and protect their wagers were a persistent problem in the sport of pedestrianism and not only at Garratt Lane. Their behaviour was a constant worry for promoters and caused the sport to be frowned on by the higher classes as only fit for ruffians.

CHAPTER 10
1858-1859
Improvements to the facility and two records

Early in December 1858 Sadler began making considerable alterations and improvements to his enclosure which *'Bell's Life'* considered would *'prove attractive to the metropolitan classes and the public at large'*. He altered the track to a circular oblong measuring 440 yards (quarter mile) in length with a 20 feet wide straight measuring 200 yards in length track for sprinting which was set diagonally across the centre of the oblong. The reduction of the original track to a quarter mile circuit simplified the lap scoring for races and having a sprint course in the centre enabled more that one event to take place at the same time if necessary. Furthermore, the reduction would increase the room available for spectators. The quarter mile (440 yards) circuit became the standard distance for athletics tracks and although nowadays altered to the equivalent metric distance of 400 metres, it remains so to the present day. It is quite possible that this change meant that the Garratt Lane track became the first track in London to adopt what then became the standard quarter mile distance of nearly all prominent athletics tracks.

Apart from the conduct of events at the track, snippets of information can be gleaned from press reports as to the layout of the Garratt Lane facility. We know that the original track was a square shape although not exactly square and that the corners were a very sharp turn. Mention is frequently made of sprinters choosing to run on the railed side of the course. The question arises as to whether this railing was on the inside or outside of the track. Mention is also made of runners, having made this decision, then having their opponent on their left which indicates that they ran around the track in an anti-clockwise direction if the rails were on the outside, or a clockwise direction if the rails were on the inside. The report of a race in October 1858 between John Phillips of Bermondsey and George Tait of Walworth describes Phillips as running next to the rails and Tait next to the hedge and in other reports this 'hedge side' is described as an 'embankment'. These descriptions would indicate that the railings were on the inside of the track not the outside and that therefore the men ran in a clockwise direction. With rails on the inside the crowds that would attend these events would therefore gather on the inside of the track and they would be 'railed in'.

The revised layout when the circuit was reduced to a quarter of a mile in the early part of 1859 possibly changed some of these arrangements. A tower type structure might have been positioned close to the finish line for the referee and umpires to gain a better view of the races and the centre of the arena could have been restricted to a select band of officials and

this would have greatly improved the view of events for spectators. What is never made entirely clear is exactly where on the circuit the finishing post was and whether it was always in the same place. It would appear that a handkerchief was attached to a finishing tape as there are many examples recorded of pedestrians breasting the handkerchief at the finish. The sprint course set up inside the track ran diagonally across the circuit and apparently ended up near the bend of the track close to a ground entrance gate. An event arranged at Wormwood Scrubs on June 13 1859 stated that all tickets that were issued for Garratt Lane, Wandsworth, will be admitted to their event. So we know that Bob Sadler had entry tickets printed for at least some of his promotions although none appear to have survived to this day.

Huge controversy surrounded a 10 miles walking handicap between William Spooner of Turnham Green and Philip Coxford of Kingsland for £50 a side on Monday December 27 with Coxford receiving the allowance of a two minute start. The agreements stated that the men were to walk fair heel and toe and the man first caught trotting would be immediately disqualified by the referee. The event was due to start at 2.00 pm but there was great difficulty in selecting a referee and just as the race was about to get underway, Coxford's backers said that they believed the chosen referee had staked money on Spooner and would not consent to their man competing while he was in charge. All parties then got involved in an angry discussion and in an attempt to appease the large and disgruntled crowd of spectators, Bob Sadler made an announcement that he would not give up any portion of the gate money until the match had been fairly decided and that when the match was rearranged there would be no charge for entry. Spooner asserted that the referee ordered him to walk over the course and having done so laid claim to the wager while Coxford denied that any referee was ever chosen. In an attempt to sort out the problem, *'Bell's Life'* ordered both parties to meet at their office in the Strand at noon on Wednesday January 5 and they called on Spooner to prove with respectable witnesses that Coxford had agreed to the referee.

On January 9 1859 *'Bell's Life'* reported:-

'The settlement of this disputed match appears to have rested on the question as to whether a referee was mutually agreed upon and a meeting was held at our office on Wednesday last to determine that point. Coxford had previously denied that he had consented to the appointment of anyone and had also stated most positively that he had never assumed his walking costume on the day. This latter statement

was abundantly disproved and sufficient evidence was produced to show that a gentlemen whose name it is not necessary for me to mention, was requested to act as referee by both parties. The award of the race therefore abides with him and his decision being in favour of Spooner, who walked over the course on the refusal of Coxford to start. We shall hand over the stakes to him on Thursday next at 12 o'clock. Bets are off'.

The New Year was hardly underway before there was more controversy. On Monday January 24 a 120 yards match had been arranged between Young Reed of Bermondsey and Richard Jackson of Walworth for £10 a side. They ran from the top end of the ground with Jackson on the right of Reed and he was therefore, nearer the embankment. The start was by mutual consent and after several attempts Reed dashed off but was not followed by Jackson who remained stationary on the scratch line. Billy Preston was attending on Reed and thinking that Jackson had gone over the scratch line called out to his man to continue running. Reed did so but did not quite breast the handkerchief marking the finishing line. Reed then claimed the stakes believing that Jackson had crossed the scratch line but the referee decided that the men must run again and return to the scratch line and on this occasion begin by the first pull of a handkerchief. An official was appointed to see a fair start and the men returned to begin again. Jackson took an early lead but with a strong finish Reed closed right up as they approached the finish. It was so close that the referee's decision was that they had run a dead heat. The referee had been employed for the task by *'Bell's Life'* and he now came under threat from a crowd of 'roughs' whose anger against him meant that the police had to intervene to prevent him suffering some bodily injury. *'Bell's Life'* was scathing at this behaviour and wrote:-

'We can only say that if respectable persons who fulfil the duties of a by no means enviable office are to be thus assailed and intimidated, the sooner pedestrianism in the neighbourhood of London is given up all together the better. The proprietors of running grounds who permit such conduct to be pursued are very much to blame. Nor can we have anything further to do with any match in which Reed is concerned except the one already announced with Anderson, for though the men themselves may not act improperly, yet they ought to have some control over the acts of their partisans and for their conduct must be held accountable'.

Twenty nine year old John Clifton, the self described 'bumble footed cripple' of Chelsea was back at Garratt Lane on February 28 to contest a 100 yards event for £5 a side against 25 year old Robert Kingsley the Bermondsey cripple who would run with the assistance of a crutch. The bookies had Kingsley as favourite at 5 to 4 and for the first 60 to 70 yards it

was a neck and neck affair. As they approached the finish Kingsley shot ahead and it was an easy decision for Bob Sadler, acting as referee, to declare him the winner by three to four yards. After reporting the race, *'Bell's Life'* took the opportunity to congratulate Bob Sadler on the improvements he had made to the track.

It was long before the days of official World or British records but a 'best time ever recorded' for 4 miles occurred on July 5 when a contest over that distance between Charles Cook of Marylebone and William Jackson *'The American Deer'* took place. It was an eagerly awaited contest as they had raced just three weeks earlier on the Hackney Wick ground when Jackson had defeated his more youthful opponent quite easily. Cook's supporters were convinced that their man could reverse the result and there was a good attendance for the race which was due to commence at 6.00 pm. It was fully an hour late when the pedestrians made their appearance and the *'Bell's Life'* report of the race later stated *'....this want of punctuality cannot be too severely censured as deceiving the public...'.* As the race got underway the odds were 5 to 4 in favour of Jackson to repeat his win and he made all the running in the early stages but his style was laboured and in marked contrast to the light and graceful Cook. The first mile passed in 4:55 but Cook moved up and took the lead on the sixth lap and by the seventh lap had a thirty yards lead on Jackson who sustained a strain in his right leg and gave up the struggle. Cook despite having no opposition, poured on the pace and came home in a fine 21:15.

Yet more controversy plagued the venue when on August 1 there was an event where Joseph Spencer a 42 year old non professional had undertaken to walk 18 miles within 3 hours. The betting at 6 to 4 demonstrated that most onlookers thought he would be unable to achieve the feat. The well known admirer of the sport Mr Bedford was appointed to officiate as referee and the equally well known George Bradshaw of Hammersmith was appointed to wait upon Spencer. Described as a strong powerfully built man, he set about his task with determination and passed through 7 miles in 1:01.35, carried on through the 15 miles mark in 2:13.35 and easily completed the 18 miles in 2:52.00 so winning his wager with eight minutes to spare. Apart from publishing a report of the race, *'Bell's Life'* also reported that they had received a letter from the appointed referee Mr Bedford stating that Spencer had not walked fairly and having been unable to stop him 'trotting', he had left the ground before the event reached its conclusion. *'Bell's Life'* final comment on the affair was:-

'We can only say that such disputes as these are very unsportsmanlike and have only one tendency – that of bringing a manly, athletic and popular pastime into disrepute among the public'.

CHAPTER 11
1859-1861
A champion walker emerges

Advertised as 'A Novice' and under the care of the well known Joseph Jenns of Somers Town, a 19 year old lad James Miles, who was living in Brixton at the time, made his competitive debut at Garratt Lane on Thursday August 11. 1859 in a 10 miles walk, competing against Fletcher of St George's. Miles won easily and *'The Era'* reported:-

'In the fifth mile the Novice coolly put on his coat and on the termination of the distance went in the winner by half a mile. Fletcher not having the remotest chance from the time his opponent left him'.

Miles was to make many more appearances at the Wandsworth track as he gained in prominence and fame in the pedestrian world. He was in fact destined to become the premier long distance walker in England.

Bob Sadler put up prizes of £10, £1 and 10/- (50p) to attract entries for a 200 yards handicap event he had arranged for Monday October 10. This would be run on his highly praised sprint course which he had built in the centre of the track and he roped and staked it into three lanes. A large crowd was attracted to come along to spectate and gamble and the entries meant that nine preliminary heats would be necessary. The races were started by gun and the nine heat winners then ran in three semi finals to decide the finalists who ended up as Alfred Crudgington of Bethnal Green off 14 yards, H Tait of Walworth off 16 yards and H Oxspring of Sheerness off 27 yards. A false start by Crudgington was penalised by him having to move 1 yard back but they got away at the second attempt and in a closely run race Oxspring came home 2 yards clear of Crudgington. Sadler had been the referee and he ruled the race to be re-run the following Saturday as some of Oxspring's supporters had got in the way of Crudgington to prevent him winning. The result of the re-run is however, not reported.

Apart from serious races there were also peculiar ones. On December 27 two men, Able and Presland were matched to race over 1000 yards for £5 a side with Able to receive a 12 yards start. The strange additional proviso was that they were both required *'to run two puncheons on their chimes'*. A 'puncheon' was a large cask capable of holding more than 100 gallons of wine and a 'chime' was the narrow hoop of iron at the end of the barrel. On the day of the race it was decided that the men could not compete on the track as it was considered not to be wide enough and that they would be unable to overtake each other, so it was decided to hold the event up and down the sprint straight turning every 150 yards until they had

completed the 1000 yards. The men began their match at 4.00 pm and it must have been quite amusing to see them manoeuvring their large upright barrels up and down the course. As far as the race was concerned, Presland soon overcame the lead Able had been allowed and went on to victory by about 12 yards.

The appearance of rising star James Miles from Brixton attracted a large crowd to the ground on January 23 when he was matched in a 10 miles walk handicap against a man called Bailey for £10 a side with Bailey having been allowed a two minute start. Without really having to extend himself, James caught his man on the second lap of the sixth mile and went on to an easy victory in 1:41.0. It was even reported that during the last portion of the race, Miles was laughing and joking with his friends in the crowd.

40) JAMES MILES (1840-?) although from East Grinstead, he was usually described as being from Brixton as he was living there when he started his outstanding career as long distance walker.

Bob Sadler had arranged a big programme for the Easter holiday weekend. On Good Friday April 6 he had put up prizes totalling £15 for a 440 yards handicap event. On the day, nine heats were run, with the semi finals and final to be run two days later on Easter Monday. Despite extremely cold weather which included showers of rain, snow and sleet, about fifteen hundred people packed into the ground to watch a 150 yards handicap event where Bob Sadler's offer of a silver snuff box and money prizes had attracted an entry which would necessitate 21 heats. Ten of these heats were run and it was decided to hold over the other eleven until April 30 so that the 440 yards handicap event from Good Friday could be finalised as well as a 1 mile race and a 4 miles walk. The leading pedestrian Frank Diamond had acted as handicapper and starter and his efforts and those of Sadler were highly praised in 'Bell's Life' who reported that:-

'The ground was in admirable order, being in all respects all that the most fastidious could require: while among the spectators, fun, good fellowship and sociability reigned supreme.'

High praise indeed from the premier sporting paper, especially considering the numerous times they had criticised the owner, the facility and the spectators in the past.

Sadly, it was a different matter a couple of weeks later following a 7 miles walk between Powling and Plumpton. The match ended in a very unsatisfactory manner when although Plumpton finished first, a full 200 yards ahead of Powling, Mr Doughty the referee refused to state on the ground whether the match had been fairly won. He and one of the umpires, a Mr Hobson, subsequently called at the 'Bell's Life' office and stated that their decision was unquestionably in favour of Powling as Plumpton had repeatedly broken into a trot. Doughty informed Bell's that he would have given his decision before leaving the ground had it not been for the threats and intimidation of Plumpton's partisans. Bell's commented:

'Such conduct as this is shameful and we are much surprised that Mr Sadler, who generally has a number of policemen in attendance, did not interfere and prevent it'.

Encouraged by the success of his Easter promotion and undeterred by more criticism, Sadler put up more prizes to be contested in another 440 yards handicap he arranged for the Whit weekend at the end of May.

At the end of April, Sadler pressed on with the eleven 150 yards handicap heats held over from Easter Monday but unfortunately, twenty of the entries did not turn up on the day so four of the heats were cancelled and a further two resulted in single runners who only had to run over the course to achieve a victory. In addition, four of the heat winners from Easter did not turn up for the second round races. So this left thirteen runners to contest the second round heats and following these, plus two semi finals and a final, J White of Aldgate came out the winner of the silver snuff box defeating J Dolman of The Guards.

Other tracks for the sport of pedestrianism were being opened in the London area and many were learning from problems encountered at tracks like Garratt Lane. The opening of 'The New Pedestrian Race Grounds' at Thistle Grove Lane in Old Brompton announced their arrival in May of 1860 by stating that all men to run in long draws and guernseys otherwise they will not be permitted to start. Also, for each man to have some distinguishing colour to be declared at the time of entry as no two colours alike will be permitted. Spectators will be railed off the grounds to allow the men to be easily seen for every yard of the race. Each man will be allowed one attendant and his backer within the rails and no more. The central part of the ground would contain a cricket pitch and additional facilities would include a forty square yards bowling green, and three racket courts. The new grounds would be under the superintendence of Mr John Roberts. The multi-sports facility was not a new idea, most of the other major pedestrian facilities in the country provided for other sports such as Wrestling, Dog racing, Rabbit Coursing, Pigeon Shooting and Quoiting and maybe Bob Sadler's ground suffered through not catering for anything other than pedestrianism.

A huge crowd was attracted to Garratt Lane on the evening of Tuesday July 3 for the return 1 mile match between James Mahoney the Irishman based in Bermondsey and Sam Barker 'The Billingsgate Boy'. Back on April 17, Mahoney had won a close 1 mile race by a couple of yards and the re-match between these two top men was eagerly anticipated. 'Bell's Life' reported that along Garratt Lane there was a continuous stream of vans, carts, cabs and traps making their way to Bob Sadler's attractive ground where inside, there was plenty of fun provided for everybody. They added that:-

'The facility presented a most pleasant, inviting and picturesque appearance, whilst the gardens attached to the grounds, were laden with the sweet perfume of the beautiful flower beds'.

They commented also that:-

'The track was in splendid condition and that while Mr Sadler has not been much patronised of late, the utmost care and attention had been bestowed on it and there was nothing that could be found fault with, that Sadler was on this occasion unremitting in his attention to all and that the manner in which he carried out the whole of the proceedings left no room for even the most captious to be dissatisfied'.

A 600 yards race and a 1 mile event preceded the main 1 mile contest. Mahoney and Barker had backed themselves at £25 each compared with the £10 a side of the first match in April. Twenty seven year old Barker had prepared for the race in Fulham, under the guidance of John Smith 'The Regent Street Pet' at his public house 'The Normand Arms' in Crown Lane. The tall, thin Mahoney, at five foot eleven inches and ten stones ten pounds contrasted sharply with the diminutive Barker who only stood five feet four inches and weighed in at seven stones eight pounds. At the appointed start time of 6.00 pm, the two men, both looking in fine condition, appeared on the ground with Barker showing as the punters favourite at 5 to 4. After a few false moves they got away and Barker immediately went into the lead which he maintained throughout the first of the four laps. Mahoney seemed unable to close up on Barker's three yard advantage throughout the second and third circuits but at the beginning of the final lap he made a really determined effort and actually drew abreast with the Billingsgate man. By now the crowd who were roaring them on, had reached a frenzy of excitement and shouts of 'Bravo Sam' 'Well done' and 'Stick to him Jem' could be heard throughout the throng. As the lap progressed, Barker gradually stole ahead and as he reached the finish he had increased his lead to some 12 yards recording 4:41.0. 'Bell's Life' reported that they had never witnessed as much excitement as was displayed by the spectators throughout this race and that Barker, amidst the most enthusiastic cheers, was almost carried off the ground. He was to remain in the sport for many years and later he would hold the 10 miles champions cup.

Another huge star of the future would be at Garratt Lane the following evening when a 19 year old Edward 'Teddy' Mills from Bethnal Green won a 1 mile handicap race despite allowing his opponent W Britton of Marylebone a twenty yard start. Teddy, who would subsequently become known as 'Young England' was to go on to become the most famous runner in the country. His range of ability was tremendous as at various times he was to hold the British 1 mile record, win the 6 miles Champion Belt and the 10 miles Champion Cup and set a British record for the 1 hour distance, running 11 miles 775 yards. This was his first year of serious competition and his appearance at Bob Sadler's ground did not attract an enormous crowd or generate the excitement in Wandsworth that the Barker v Mahoney clash had generated twenty four hours earlier.

On Thursday October 4, Mills was back at Garratt Lane to run in a 880 yards handicap against J Lord to whom he had allowed a 20 yards start. Bob Sadler was the referee, his decision was a dead heat and the stakes of £5 a side were mutually agreed to be withdrawn. The third appearance of Mills at Garratt Lane was on Tuesday November 5 where he faced

41) Bethnal Green's TEDDY MILLS 'Young England' (1841-1894), who first ran at the Garratt Lane track in 1860 aged 19 and who later became the outstanding long distance runner in England.

Sam Barker from Billingsgate for £25 a side, in a 2 miles handicap race with Mills being allowed a 50 yard start. A well contested race was fully expected and these expectations were completely realised. For some reason it was decided not to start in the usual place but would happen on the opposite side of the course than normal. Eight laps of the track would be necessary from wherever they had started so it is not clear why the change was made. During the race Mills would be looked after by Bill Price while Barker was in the care of John Smith, 'The Regent Street Pet'. Both men in turn became favourites and although betting opened at 6 to 4 on the Billingsgate champion, Mills supporters were still quite prepared to back their man and the final quote for the betting was 6 to 4 on Mills. When the men took up their starting positions and the gun set them off, Mills went away at a tremendous pace and after three laps had increased his lead from 50 to 80 yards. Barker however was a quality runner and as the second mile started he began to eat away at Mills lead so that as they reached the point 150 yards from the finish he actually took the lead amidst deafening cheers. In that last 150 yards battle for supremacy Mills rallied, once again regained the lead and at the finish came in 4 yards ahead. His winning time of 9:55 showed that Barker must have run a very fine 9:57 for the full distance.

A large assembly was again at the ground for a 4 miles walking match between Brixton's James Miles and Poplar's John Hotine on Monday December 3 and 'Bell's Life' had requested that Bob Sadler be the referee for the race. The unfavourable weather had left the course in a heavy condition but at the start Miles immediately went into a lead and his clean walking style sharply contrasted with the crude walking method of Hotine. The agreed rule was that only one warning would be given if either man was not considered to be walking fairly and Sadler issued this warning to Hotine during the sixth lap. It made absolutely no difference to Hotine's method of progress and Sadler cautioned him repeatedly. Sadler's patience ran out on the eleventh lap when both men were approaching two and three quarter miles he told Hotine that he was disqualified and then left the ground. Despite his disqualification, Hotine did not drop out but continued to chase Miles who then decided to put on the pressure and at the end of the 4 miles was 60 yards ahead of his disqualified opponent in 31:07.

Following the demolition of 'The Old Cope' in Islington for the building of the new cattle market, John Garratt the owner had not fared well and had in December 1860 been declared penniless. His many friends in the sport decided that a benefit should be arranged on his behalf and Bob Sadler was one of the organising committee alongside James Baum proprietor of the 'Hackney Wick Track', John Roberts

of the 'West London Cricket Ground, Brompton', Thomas Wilson of 'The Spotted Dog' in the Strand, Fred Chandler of 'The Red Lion', Blackman Street, Borough, where the various cups on offer could be viewed, Mr Sillman of 'The White Horse', Fann Street, Aldersgate and in addition Mr Burnman, Bill Price and Bill Preston.

They decided on a programme of events to be held at the Hackney Wick track on Monday April 11 1861 starting at 1.00 pm and it attracted many of the prominent pedestrians. Pugilism was closely connected with pedestrianism and Tom Sayers the heavyweight champion as well as Jem Mace the middleweight champion promised to attend. The occasion and the high standard of the contestants attracted three and a half thousand spectators.

Events continued on a regular basis at Garratt Lane and a strange event occurred on Thursday May 30 when a match over 170 yards had been arranged between two amateurs John Collier and John Abrahams. The previous month they had attempted to race in Northampton but on the day named it had been impossible to bring the race to a satisfactory conclusion owing to a variety of circumstances. The men had asked 'Bell's Life' to make the necessary arrangements to get the match held and both men put up £55 as the stake. About a hundred spectators, many of whom were personal friends of the men, had come to London the previous day for the Derby and then stayed on to be present at the match. 'Bell's Life' said that they had never seen the ground in finer condition and that it bore ample proof of the care and attention bestowed on it. The men appeared on the track just after 6.00 pm and the appointed referee told them that he had requested Bob Sadler to be the starter and that if they had not started by mutual agreement after 15 minutes he would use a gun to start the race. The referee took up his position at the finish and left the starting arrangements to Sadler who stood with his watch in hand while the men made some abortive but not convincing attempts to start. After 15 minutes he informed the men that he would now start them with the pistol and took up a position behind them as they toed the scratch line. When the gun was fired Collier took off but Abrahams, to the amazement of the spectators, did not make the slightest move. Collier completed the distance totally unchallenged and the referee, having spoken to Sadler to confirm the fairness of the start, awarded the £110 stake to him. Before leaving the ground he declared that all bets were off but in the following weeks' 'Bell's Life' they stated that as stakeholders they had received notice not to pay over the stakes but upon them getting a sufficient guarantee against legal expenses that they would pay over the money to Collier and so ended a very odd affair.

CHAPTER 12
1861-1862

The arrival of Deerfoot to England with George Martin and John Garratt takes over by renaming the ground

The former sprinter George Martin had now become a leading promoter of pedestrian events. Born in Blackwater, on the Hampshire Berkshire border in 1826, he was the son of local shoemaker James Martin and his wife Prudence. Although like his father he trained as a shoemaker, in 1844 aged 18 he made the decision to take running seriously, He moved to London and came under the care of Ned Smith *'The West End Runner'* who with his brother John Smith *'The Regent Street Pet'* had a stable of promising Pedestrians who they trained and they operated from *'The White Hart'* in Drury Lane. Martin's own performances as a pedestrian were not inconsiderable and certainly were not without controversy. Negative press reports about him illegally entering competitions and a two month remand for bankruptcy both featured in his early career as a pedestrian. By 1848 he was living in Sunderland, issuing challenges and successfully competing in sprinting and hurdling events.

The following year he established a friendship with James Holden the proprietor of *'The White Lion'* in Long Millgate, Manchester. He had also established a friendship with James's daughter Alice, so much so, that he decided to relocate to Manchester in 1851 when on January 14 they were married at St John's church in that city. A couple of months later he followed a path trodden by many successful sportsmen by becoming the proprietor of *'The Plasterer's Arms'* in Gregson Street, Deansgate. In 1852, James, the first of his six children was born. Because of George's frequent family relocations between Manchester and London three were born in each city.

It was a tragic occurrence when in 1854 George's father James, suffering from mental illness,

committed suicide after he had murdered George's mother Prudence. George moved to London to arrange the funeral and to manage the shoemaking business. He was living in Little Windmill Street, Westminster and he continued to compete regularly himself, which included appearances at the Garratt Lane track. He had begun to train others when first in Manchester and he was back there again in 1858 when, just after he had filed for bankruptcy for the second time, he announced his retirement as an active athlete to concentrate more on training and promoting the sport. His skill as a publicist and promoter was within a few years to earn him the title of *'The wizard of Pedestrianism'.*

George's idea of taking some of his training group to compete in America resulted in him seeing the potential of a tall native American Indian Louis Bennett also known as Deerfoot and realising the possibility of introducing this man to the English pedestrian scene, Martin persuaded him to accompany the group on their return journey to England. The group left New York on Saturday July 27 aboard the steamship *'City of Washington'.* The very rough twelve day journey reached its conclusion when they disembarked at Liverpool on Thursday August 8 1861. Travelling on down to London, George Martin booked Deerfoot into *'The Spotted Dog'* in the Strand opposite the offices of *'Bell's Life'.* This placed him at the centre of the pedestrian scene in the capital.

The Sunday August 11 issue of *'Bell's Life'* carried a small announcement but its repercussions were going to have an enormous effect on English pedestrianism and bring a level of excitement to the sport that had never been witnessed before. The announcement read:-

42) GEORGE MARTIN (1826-1865), a former pedestrian himself who became known as *'The wizard of Pedestrianism'* for his outstanding ability as a promoter.

'An Indian of Catterangus, North America, known by the name of Deerfoot and Red Jacket, has visited England for the purpose of testing the fleet powers of our pedestrians and aims at nothing lower than the 10 miles Champion Cup and the 6 miles Champion Belt. Ready to make a match at each distance, he has left £10 with us and the acceptor has only to cover this sum and meet the Indian (or his representative) at Mr Wilson's Spotted Dog on Friday next and the match will go on'.

The announcement got an immediate response from England's top men with James Pudney, Teddy Mills and John Brighton all responding that they would be happy to race against the 'Red Indian'.

Bringing Deerfoot to England was a master stroke of opportunism that ignited the sport of pedestrianism and for the Victorian public provided a spectacle that they would never forget. The native American was a tall well built man while most of the English runners were small if not diminutive. Deerfoot would often precede his races with a parade around the race track dressed in a wolf skin and when he stripped down for the race, it would be seen that he wore only the traditional native American costume and a belt with bells attached that would jingle as he ran With a feather secured in his headband and moccasins on his feet, he was also capable of 'war whoops' at his moment of victory which all added to the colour and excitement of the occasion.

To maximise his investment, George Martin was anxious for Deerfoot to race as often as possible and he was soon challenging and usually beating the leading English runners. Before the end of 1861, he had competed in Hackney, Brompton, Sheffield, Birmingham, Manchester, Southsea, Leeds, Cambridge, Norwich and Great Yarmouth as well as travelling to Dublin for two races.

This introduction to England of a native American pedestrian, led to a tremendous boom in the sport but would also be a major cause of bringing the sport into disrepute. Wandsworth was later to be the stage where charges against Martin would be heard in a court of law.

The week following the announcement of Deerfoot's arrival, *'Bell's Life'* carried another announcement of an intended match at Garratt Lane between Jem Mace the middleweight boxing champion of England and F Oliver the son of Tom Oliver the pugilist. They were matched to run 50 yards for £5 a side at 6.00 pm on Saturday August 24. It is sad to relate that Jem, the

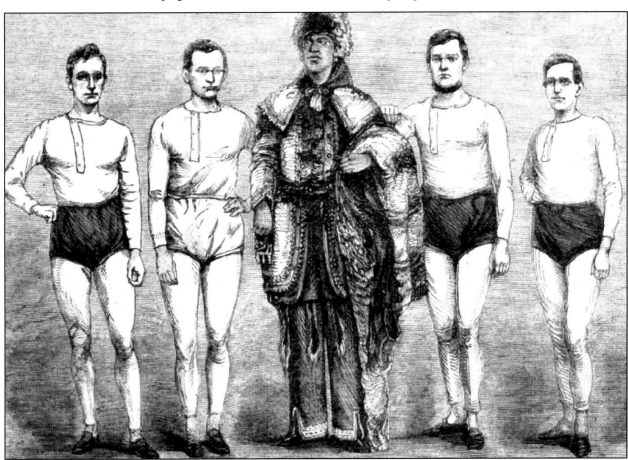

43) A group of pedestrians on the occasion of a race at Cambridge on December 4 1861 which was held in the presence of the Prince of Wales. From left to right:- TEDDY MILLS, JOHN BRIGHTON, DEERFOOT, WILLIAM LANG and SAM BARKER.

man who would become known as *'the father of modern boxing'* forfeited his £5 deposit and the match did not come off. Apparently, Mace who was no mean runner himself, had a strong interest in the sport and was often in attendance at pedestrian events throughout the country. Apart from competing himself he particularly supported the races featuring his friend Teddy Mills *'Young England'*.

Bob Sadler was involved in another starting fiasco on Saturday October 12 when he was acting in the capacity of referee. Following the opening event over 120 yards which was concluded in a satisfactory manner, there was a 200 yards match between Rowland and Croby. Sadler appointed the same man to conduct the start, instructing him to first ascertain that the men were in the correct position and ready to commence. Unfortunately the official on walking towards the men and still at a distance of some 20 yards away from them fired the gun and while Rowland bounded off into the distance, Croby stayed firmly at the start line. Rowland's supporters considered their man should have been awarded the stake but Sadler on questioning the starter ruled that it had not been a fair start and ordered the race to be re-run with a new man taking on the starting role. The race was run again and despite his earlier efforts, Rowland came in the winner by some 10 yards.

For some time it had been apparent that the pedestrian grounds in Garratt Lane were in something of a decline. Matches were still arranged on a regular basis but usually they were just single events and they invariably only attracted a small assembly of the men's supporters. The White Lion Grounds at Hackney Wick had become the premier track in London, was more easily accessible by public transport and attracted huge crowds as well as the best runners. James Baum, the landlord of *'The White Lion'* and Bill Price the manager of the track attached to it, were two very well respected men within the sport. Price was also a promoter and coach and

44) THE PRINCE OF WALES (1841-1910) was a student at Trinity College, Cambridge at the time he witnessed Derfoot running there in 1861.

45) The champion boxer of England JEM MACE (1831-1910), who although due to run at the Garratt Lane track was unable to do so but possibly attended many of the events held there.

he had a number of the top men in his stable. Also, whereas Bob Sadler had only ever promoted running and walking events at Garratt Lane, many other tracks used their arenas for other purposes and often held meetings where spectators were quite happy be treated to the variety of having more than one sport to watch and wager on.

It seemed obvious that something was afoot when a notice in *'Bell's Life'* on December 8 under the heading *'Garratt Lane, Wandsworth'*, stated that it was the intention of a gentleman to give £10 for a 2 miles handicap and Silver Cup for a 150 yards sprint handicap to be held in Christmas week. Entries could be made at Mr Chandler's *'Red Lion'*, Blackman Street, Borough, Jesse Smith's *'Proud Peacock'* in Maiden Lane and Mr Wilson's *'Spotted Dog'* in the Strand. It added that days would be set aside for shooting, rabbit coursing, wrestling etc., For once there was mention of other sports taking place at the ground and for the first time, no mention whatsoever of Robert Sadler.

All became clear the following week. It appeared that John Garratt's finances had improved sufficiently for him to take over the *'New Surrey Pedestrian Ground'* from Sadler and he would immediately rename it *'The Copenhagen Running Grounds'* presumably in memory of the track he had managed so successfully in Islington. It is quite strange that several other running tracks also used the *'Copenhagen'* name. One at Shepherds Bush had been opened in 1856, one at Newton Heath, Manchester in 1857, another in North London at Islington the same year and yet another at Holloway in 1861. Garratt announced his determination to turn the facility into the headquarters of pedestrianism and athletic training. Within two months he had made a number of improvements including railing the course and building both new shower baths and changing rooms. *'Bells Life'* further praised the medical properties of the celebrated artesian well on the premises and stated that the running ground had long been acknowledged to be one of the best in England having just recently been improved and was now in first class order.

On December 14 just as the new arrangements were being finalised, Queen Victoria's husband Prince Albert died aged only 42 and all sporting events planned for Monday December 23 were cancelled as a mark of respect for his funeral taking place that day. John Garratt's first events in charge were on Boxing Day, Thursday December 26 1861 when handicaps were run over 150 yards and a 2 miles walk which featured the well known walker William Hatley.

The following day the first competitive pigeon shooting event was held with two sweepstakes at seven birds each shoot. It was announced that shooting days at the ground would in future be fixed on a Thursday. In much the same way as the pedestrian events, matches were arranged for monetary stakes with betting amongst the spectators. The birds, usually pigeons or sparrows, were released from traps and there would be rules regarding the weight of shot and the type of gun to be used which appeared normally to be double barrelled shotguns. Following these events the shooting party would often sit down to a slap up meal presumably at 'The Wellington Inn'.

On January 9 1862 for the event due to start at 1.00 pm, the prize to be shot for was a fat pig and the rules were five birds to be released, 21 yards rise, 1 ½ oz of shot, all to load from one bowl. The event however, did not happen as it was discovered that following some sweepstakes and practice before the appointed hour, that there were not sufficient birds left and the large crowd who had assembled were asked to come back the following Tuesday when Mr Hammond would supply more birds.

On Monday January 13 John Garratt put on a 440 yards handicap over 10 hurdles and a surprise entry was William Lang of Middlesborough who successfully won his heat followed by the final which was not held until the following day. Lang was to become one of England's premier runners with outstanding performances from 1 mile run in 4:17 ¼ to 11 miles 871y completed in 1 hour and although his winning time was not recorded on this occasion it is interesting that at this stage of his career he should be running in a rather obscure hurdles event so far from his home.

The official opening day for John Garratt's new facility was to be Tuesday February 25 1862 but even before that date, Garratt had agreed with George Martin for the citizens of Wandsworth to be treated to a sight of the man who had become the talk of London. George Martin and possibly Deerfoot, had taken up residence

in the little village of Garratt just a couple of hundred yards up the road from the track. The American had been engaged to compete in his first race of 1862, a 6 miles event, against Manchester's Job Smith and it was to take place at John Garratt's ground on Monday February 17 for a £50 cash prize. Job Smith arrived down from Manchester and arranged to stay the weekend with Jesse Smith at 'The Proud Peacock' in Maiden Lane. Smith would accompany him down to Wandsworth and look after his needs during the forthcoming race. Smith had run twice previously at the track but that was back in 1858 when the circuit had been three laps to the mile so this would be his first experience on the new arena.

Posters for the event were produced with an illustration of Deerfoot depicted in his Indian running costume. The poster claimed the ground could accommodate 30,000 spectators with an arena to allow for a further 5,000. The sleepy little communities in Garratt and Summerstown would be invaded as every quarter of an hour trains from London Bridge, Waterloo and Victoria would convey passengers to Wandsworth Town station. Admission to the ground would be a shilling (5p) with reserved places extra and while John Garratt's staff collected the entrance fees, Bob Sadler and his wife Sarah would welcome them to their 'Wellington Inn' and tea gardens and for sixpence (2½p).would allow them into the temporary stand he had erected so as to view over into the running track.

The race had been arranged for 4.00 pm and it was some fifteen minutes later that Deerfoot and Smith appeared on the track accompanied by their managers, George Martin for Deerfoot and Jesse Smith for Job Smith. Deerfoot was dressed in his Indian costume complete with headband and feather while Smith wore crimson draws over his traditional pedestrian costume. The former sprinter now turned journalist Harry Reed had been designated as referee and he soon got the race underway. It was unfortunately damp and drizzly which restricted the attendance to about 2,000. Deerfoot had not competed for two months and must have welcomed the opportunity to stretch his legs in competition. The early pace was fast as both runners took turns to lead, passing 1 mile in 4:55, 2 miles in 9:57 and 3 miles in 15:19. By the fourth mile however, Deerfoot had opened up a 25 yards lead passing in 21:42. As he steadily increased his lead, Smith looked more and more a beaten man. At the four and a half miles mark he was 50 yards in arrears, at this point his manager Jesse Smith told him to call it a day and he walked off the track leaving the Indian to complete the distance on his own. Deerfoot passed the 5 miles mark in 26:02 and finished the 6 miles in a casual 32:26 to pick up the £50 stake.

46) The poster advertising the match between DEERFOOT and JOB SMITH at the Garratt Lane track on February 17 1862. (courtesy of Wandsworth Heritage Service).

47) When stripped and ready for action, the tall DEERFOOT (1830-1896) must have been an enormously impressive and intriguing sight to Victorian spectators all over Britain.

Tuesday February 25 arrived which was the appointed official 'Opening Day' for the newly named track and John Garratt had arranged a fine bill of fare. Unfortunately though, the weather was bitterly cold which had an adverse effect on the attendance but those that were present and had paid their shilling (5p) entrance, were provided with a veteran's handicap of 80 yards where amongst the competitors were John Roberts the proprietor of 'The Brompton Running Grounds' and Jesse Smith the proprietor of 'The Proud Peacock', a 4 miles walking handicap and the main event of a 6 miles running handicap which had attracted some of the best runners in England including Teddy Mills off the scratch mark, John Brighton off 25 yards. Sam Barker off 160 yards, Job Smith off 250 yards, while William Newman, Toddy Ray and Harry Andrews were all off 660 yards Perry and Hodgson off 880 yards and Shaver off 1000 yards. Mills, who was rapidly becoming the finest runner in the country, cut down the lead of all those in front of him to come in victorious in 31 minutes 20 seconds. It was even more remarkable as it was the second of three races he was to run on consecutive days having won a 4 miles race at Hackney Wick the previous day and before winning another 4 miles race in Oxford the following day. In a social event,

presumably held in 'The Wellington' that evening, John Garratt presented gold medals to the winners of the three events and the health and happiness of Mr Garratt and his family were drunk with great cordiality and with the most hearty wishes for his success at 'The Copenhagen Grounds', Wandsworth.

There was an amazing £10 a side event held on March 24 when William Priestley of Bermondsey was matched to compete against William Myers of Newmarket to race over 500 three feet six inch hurdles set 10 yards apart with rules that stated if either man knocked down a hurdle he must put it back up and jump it again. The match was closely contested until the completion of the third lap when Myers began to fall further behind Priestley and at the end of the seventh lap decided to retire from the contest as he was now 20 hurdles behind Priestley who carried on to complete the task and claim the £20 stakes. William Priestley must have been a hardy and dogged pedestrian particularly when it is remembered that he had frequently run at the Garratt Lane ground even as far back as 1853 when in its first year of operation.

John Garratt's fortune with the local Justices of the Peace was no better than Bob Sadler's had been and his application for a victuallers licence in March 1862 was refused having been opposed by David Palmer of 'The Prince of Wales' and Philip Fenton of 'The Leather Bottle' who were both operating nearby in Garratt Lane. It appears however, that Bob Sadler and his family still retained some interest in the property and that it was only the running track that he had been passed over to John Garratt.

48) WILLIAM MYERS of Newmarket (left) and WILLIAM PRIESTLEY of Bermondsey (right) who contested an amazing race over five hundred hurdles at Garratt Lane in March 1862.

CHAPTER 13
1862
A Summer of Miles

On Monday April 14 a 10 miles walk championship race had been set up to compete for a newly produced belt. Prior to the event, the belt, worth £20, would be exhibited at Fred Chandler's *'Red Lion'* in the Borough, Mr Wilson's *'Spotted Dog'* in the Strand and at *'The Copenhagen Grounds'* Wandsworth. The winner would have to agree to defend it and accept all challenges on the handicap terms for £25 a side within six weeks, or else forfeit the belt. Should he defend it successfully for eighteen months, the belt would become his own property. A good field was assembled for the event with 20 starters including top men James Miles of Brixton and Joseph Oliver of Pimlico while Charles Westhall was appointed as the referee. After the first 6 miles the twenty man field had been reduced to only six through retirements or disqualifications. The large crowd present loudly cheered Miles to a fine victory in 1:27.17 ahead of Thomas of Shrewsbury, who had received a 2 minute start, in 1:28.47.

By early April, George Martin had announced in *'The Illustrated Sporting News'* that his address was now Catterangus Villa, Garratt Lane, near Tooting, Surrey and all communications respecting engagements for Deerfoot should be sent to him there. It is not known exactly where this villa was and neither is it absolutely clear if Deerfoot was staying there with him but it is highly possible that he was, as Martin would have wanted to keep a close eye on his main source of income. By now Martin had five children with the sixth Alice on the way, it is to be assumed that his wife and the growing family were also with him in the Garratt Lane villa.

Deerfoot continued to race regularly but George Martin fully realising the pulling power of his athlete, was determined to capitalise on his investment to the full. He gathered a group of runners together including William Jackson. Charles Mower, John Brighton, Harry Andrews, and William Lang and embarked on a tour the length and breath of Britain. So as to be able to charge admission, they travelled with portable fencing and canvas that could be easily erected wherever they chose to race. Martin claimed that he was capable of erecting an arena twelve foot high and nearly a quarter of a mile in circumference. Between May 7 and June 20 they ran 4 miles races in thirty seven towns. After a 16 day break, when Martin and Deerfoot moved back to the villa in Garratt Lane, the tour recommenced on July 8 and from then until September 10 over forty more races were organised in England, Scotland and Ireland. This was a quite incredible schedule of travelling and racing considering that apart from some rail travel, the primary method of transport was still the horse and cart and they had to continually load and unload their portable fencing.

A match had been arranged for Monday May 26 between James Miles and Joseph Oliver to walk 8 miles for the huge sum of £100 a side , the largest wager ever competed for at the ground, with Oliver receiving a minute and a half start. Both men had gone into strict training with Miles doing most of his work at Garratt Lane under the guidance of William Lang, while Oliver did his preparation at Ewell while based at *'The Jolly Waggoner'*. Early deposits of the stakes were made at *'Mr Bignell's Stores'* in Jermyn Street and when the final deposits were due at Mr Lowry's, *'Old Queen's Head'*, Stockwell, they attracted the attendance of a very large company of sporting gentleman. Betting already had commenced in earnest and some hundreds were laid out at £60 to £50 on Miles with one large bookmaker laying a bet of £140 to £100 that neither man would walk the 8 miles within one hour.

49) JOSEPH OLIVER (1839- ?) from Pimlico was a worthy opponent for the outstanding walker James Miles.

The day arrived and prior to the main event, Charles Sutton, an amateur of Upper Tooting, who was apparently supported by Mr Day the landlord of 'The Kings Head' in Tooting had undertaken to run 10 miles in less than seventy minutes and he easily achieved his goal coming home in 62:30 to win his wager in a very easy manner The crowd was gathering during this feat and by the time Oliver and Miles were due to start their £200 match, something in excess of two thousand people had arrived at the ground. Mr Thomas, a pigeon shooting celebrity, had been appointed referee, William Lang was to be the attendant for Miles while Oliver was to be waited on by Rubens and J Oliver while Bill Price, the manager of the Hackney Wick ground, was chosen to be the official timekeeper. The race had been due to start at 6.30 pm but by the time the preliminaries had been sorted out it was nearer 7.00 pm when Mr Thomas sent Oliver on his way and during his one and a half minutes start allowance, he completed 400 yards so

that as Miles started he was already almost a lap behind. James set about his work in impressive style and immediately began to eat into Oliver's lead, covering the first mile in 7:57. By the time Miles had completed five miles in 41:51, he had reduced Oliver's lead to about 140 yards and as he finished the seventh mile in 58:09, Oliver's lead was only 40 yards. Miles hit the front on the bottom bend during the thirtieth lap and in the remaining two laps, increased this to reach the finish line 20 yards ahead with Bill Price's watch showing 1:08.37.

Whit Monday June 9 saw Miles back at Garratt Lane to contest a 14 miles walk against the champion William Spooner. Miles would be trying to avenge a defeat over the same distance he had suffered at the hands, or rather feet, of Spooner at the Brompton track back in February. On this occasion he would be given an allowance of 1 minute and when the referee John Garratt set him off he traversed 300 yards in his allotted start and before Spooner was allowed to set

50) This is the only known illustration of an event at the Copenhagen Grounds, Garratt Lane. It appeared in 'The Illustrated Sporting News' on May 31 1862 and again in the same newspaper of December 23 1865. It depicts the 8 Miles walking match between JAMES MILES and JOSEPH OLIVER held on May 26 1862 where both men had wagered £100 each as the prize money which was the largest ever stake competed for at the ground. The crowd are held back behind a stout fence and Miles is attended on by William Lang. No doubt the ground's proprietor John Garratt, the referee Mr Thomas and the timekeeper Bill Price are shown amongst those close to the finish. The apparent ruins of a building at the back of the illustration are a mystery but the drawing clearly shows the extreme narrowness of the track and the close proximity and obvious excitement of the spectators. The illustration skilfully coloured by Fay Whiting is reproduced again on the book cover.

out after him. After 4 miles, which Miles covered in 31:12, his lead had been reduced to 16 seconds and by 6 miles had been further reduced to just 10 seconds. From this point onwards Spooner made no further inroad on the lead and by the halfway point of twenty eight laps Miles had regained a 30 yards lead which he continued to increase and half way through the ninth mile Spooner retired from the contest dead beat leaving Miles to finish the allotted distance at his leisure. He obviously suffered no ill effects as the following day he was back to carry of a silver cup by winning a 4 miles walk handicap from the scratch mark.

At the end of June, an old pedestrian Mountjoy had a severe accident when he was attacked by a bull somewhere in Wandsworth. He suffered severe injuries breaking several ribs and having his collar bone and breast bone both injured. John Garratt having obviously known him as an active athlete took him in to his house in Garratt Lane to recover and

51) MOUNTJOY the former Pedestrian injured by a bull in Wandsworth in 1862.

'Bell's Life' set up a subscription to alleviate his sufferings and directed contributions towards John Garratt and to Thomas Wilson at 'The Spotted Dog' in the Strand. In addition, an event was arranged for Tuesday August 12 at the Copenhagen Grounds to help him as was now in a destitute condition.

Miles was back on Monday July 27 to contest a 10 miles handicap against Joseph Oliver and George Davis of Battersea. Each man had put up £25 and Miles had added in his champion's belt. Miles had allowed Davis a two minute start and Oliver one and a half minutes. John Garratt was the timekeeper and just after 7.00 pm he set Davis on his way with Oliver going off thirty seconds later. The watch having run for two minutes, Miles was then sent on his way and immediately began to gain on the others but after he had walked 5 miles and having gained some 200 yards but still 400 yards behind Davis, he suddenly ceased walking complaining of a severe stitch in his right side which made it impossible for him to continue. It surprised all present when Oliver having walked 8 miles also pulled up leaving Davis to continue the match at his leisure and to successfully carry off the £75 stakes and the champion's belt.

John Garratt and Jesse Smith had hoped to promote a 150 yards gentleman's handicap on Saturday August 9 and had already started accepting entries at 7/6 (37 1/2p) each. They intended having a very select attendance for the contest charging a shilling (5p) for entry which would be by ticket only to keep it 'select', but the event had to be unavoidably postponed on account of the commencement of the grouse shooting season as many of the gentlemen entered, not being professional pedestrians, wished to visit the moors and therefore would be unable to devote sufficient time to train properly.

A crowd approaching 2000 made there way along Garratt Lane and poured into the ground on Monday August 11 to witness whether 22 year old James Miles could achieve a performance only previously done by Charles Westhall in walking 21 miles in under 3 hours. Westhall's feat had been achieved on Newmarket Heath back in February 1857 with just less than a minute to spare but had never been achieved on a measured track. The backer of Miles and the backer of 'Time', the bookmaker Charles Wale and James Handley stood to win £100 as the stakes were £50 a side. Just after 4.00 pm Miles, came out on the ground wrapped in a small blanket while the referee and timekeepers took up their position at a table in the centre of the ground with the watches protected securely under a glass case. At five minutes to five Miles was on the scratch line and when the pistol signalled him to start he went away displaying his neat and completely fair walking style which drew admiration from the knowledgeable crowd. He rattled along going through 5 miles in 41:36 and 10 in 1:25.05. The first sign of some distress came on the first lap of the thirteenth mile when he stopped just briefly to massage his side before continuing on and he recorded 2:10.33 as he went past 15 miles. It was now apparent that he was beginning to fall behind the necessary schedule but he struggled gamely on and was at the bend at the bottom end of the course on the first lap of the seventeenth mile when he reeled and fell to the ground and had to be carried from the course by his supporters and it was not until he had been put to bed that he became fully conscious again.

Miles still felt he could achieve the performance and he soon made another attempt at Garratt Lane with the walk arranged for Monday September 29. Before the end of August, Miles was challenged by a prominent northern walker, James Seel of Staleybridge, to defend his 10 miles belt which, although Miles had lost to Battersea's George Davis, he had won back by forfeit. Miles replied that he was quite willing to race but it would have to be two weeks after his 21 miles record attempt.

For his second attempt to walk 7 miles an hour for 3 successive hours on September 29 Miles prepared under the supervision of Ben Mason of Clapham and to further assist his attempt, he had taken up residence with John Garratt and was training on the Garratt Lane track on a daily basis. In the pre race publicity it was stated that:-

'No one under any pretence whatever will be allowed in the enclosure except for the Referee, Timekeepers and members of the press. Each and all the visitors will thus have a fair chance of seeing and Miles himself allowed a 'fair field and no favour' in his great trial for the mastery over his powerful opponent 'Time' the unerring one'.

Unfortunately rain had fallen throughout the two days leading up to the event and on the day itself it was cold, wet and gloomy. *'The Illustrated Sporting News'* commented that on arrival at the grounds and expecting to see the track in poor condition they were surprised at the good condition in which they found it and stated that this could not have been achieved without considerable outlay on drainage and preparation of the surface.

Admission to the ground was sixpence (2 1/2p) with reserved places extra and odds of £50 to £25 were been laid by Bill Price that Miles could not achieve the feat. The incessant rain had reduced the attendance to some 200 but more arrived once the event was underway and by the finish it was in excess of 600. For some reason it was calculated that Miles would have to cover 84 laps less 70 yards. The four watches that were to be used belonged to

52) JAMES SEEL the prominent walker from Staleybridge.

John Garratt, Bill Price and the pedestrians May and Reed and were placed in the official box with the glass lid to enable them to seen as working properly. In deciding the final arrangements, it was agreed that it would be Price's watch that would be the official timer and only his watch and Garratt's were left in the box as the event got underway at 3.00 pm.

The odds were 3 to 1 on 'Time' mainly due to the very poor weather. Miles was being looked after throughout by 'Young Smith' of Bermondsey and his walking style was admired by all present, which included the record holder Charles Westhall, as stylish and totally fair. He was three minutes ahead of the necessary schedule as he went through 7 miles in 57 minutes and was still to the good as the half way point of 10½ miles was passed in 1:27.0 as the rain continued to come down in a pitiless manner. At 14 miles passed in 1:57.11, he was still 2:49 in hand to achieve the task and it was not until this point that Smith supplied him with his first sip of refreshment. Going through 19 miles in 2:42.33, there were the first signs that he was beginning to labour as on some portions of the course his stride appeared to shorten and his attendant continually threw water on his chest and legs to ease his pain. The nearer the match approached its climax, the more intense became the excitement and the cheering of his supporters was louder and louder. As James entered the eighty fourth and final lap, the referee announced the time and during the final minute called it out second by second to prevent the possibility of mistake. Despite the most strenuous efforts of Miles as the referee shouted 'Time's up' he fell just short of his goal and did not pass the 21 miles mark until just 10 seconds after the 3 hour time limit. His gallant effort in the very poor weather conditions had been a failure but his performance had gained the utmost admiration of all present and was considered to be one of the greatest walking feats of all time.

James's next pedestrian task was to defend his champion belt and £50 stake in a match against James Seel of Staleybridge when Miles was required by the agreement to give his opponent a one and a half minute start in a 10 miles handicap. Seel arrived in London with his trainer on Friday October 3 and took up residence at Jesse Smith's 'Proud Peacock' in Maiden Lane. A large crowd was anticipated on the day and so it proved as on Monday October 13 over 1000 arrived at the track having poured in from Waterloo and Pimlico stations hoping to witness a great contest. 'The Illustrated Sporting News' complained that it was a tedious distance from the station to the ground; that the cab drivers were making the most of the distance and the foul weather by increasing their fares by fifty percent and the dreadful condition of Garratt Lane itself mainly due to the inclement weather.

Leading pedestrian Jack White 'The Gateshead Clipper', was noticed amongst the many interested spectators and was seen to be timing each circuit and marking off the laps. Despite the allowance given to Seel, Miles was the favourite according to the bookies and many punters were prepared to put their money on him. Proprietor John Garratt was seen to be confined to his box and using crutches for what was described as a 'most malignant disorder' and as the evening was getting darker and the advertised starting time of 4.00 pm had long passed he was urged to get the event underway. A bell was tolled to summon the pedestrians to the track and both men made their appearance sheltered underneath umbrellas and went around the track to the cheers of their supporters, Seel under the care of Fred Oliver while Miles was once again looked after by Bermondsey's 'Young Smith'. Seel then stripped for action and got a quick rub down and then amused Miles and his supporters by walking out for a hundred yards or so as a means of warming up and displayed a peculiar walking style, his strides were heavy and short, his head and body bent forward and his arms flapped in an ungainly manner. He was said to resemble a bustling little city gentleman wending his way down Cheapside rather than a top pedestrian and his method of progress was certainly going to contrast greatly with the upright and stylish action of the Brixton man. The race then got underway and in his ninety second advantage, Seel covered 400 yards before Miles was set on his way. James immediately began to cut into Seel's lead and continued to do so and by 6 miles Seel's lead had been reduced to just 100 yards. Within the next couple of miles, the margin was reduced to just 50 yards but then Miles begun to show signs of distress and at the end of the eighth mile virtually collapsed, despite his attendant Smith grabbing a bottle of water from one of the umpires and dashing the contents into his face. Miles complaining of blindness was compelled to resign and was led away in a deplorable condition. As he was led off the ground by his helpers, Seel completed the distance unopposed to claim both the belt and the £50 stakes. The general opinion was that Miles's supreme effort in the match against 'Time' only fourteen days earlier, had left him somewhat weakened.

His huge popularity however, was still intact and Bill Price announced that he had arranged a benefit for him to take place at the Hackney Wick track on November 10 and he urged all who admire such doings, pluck and stamina to give their support for the good of the beaten man, while James Seel immediately offered a fresh match over 10 miles on Saturday November 22 to come off at the Bradford New Ground near Manchester with the belt and £25 a side being the stakes and for Miles to allow him the same one and a half minutes start.

CHAPTER 14
1862-1863

The court case at Wandsworth County Court and Deerfoot's extraordinary second race at the Copenhagen Grounds

William Jackson *'The American Deer'* had participated in George Martin's Deefoot tour but was now past his best as a pedestrian and had finished last or next to last in most of the races on the tour, he now claimed that George Martin still owed him at least £6 in unpaid wages. Unable to extract the money from Martin, he took the matter to court and Thursday October 23 1862 was the date set for the hearing and The County Court at the Wandsworth end of Garratt Lane was the scene for the dramatic case to be heard by Judge Frazer.

Under his real name of William Howitt, he gave evidence that Martin had failed to pay him the wages he had been promised. In response, Martin claimed he had no memory of any amounts outstanding and had not brought his business papers with him as it would have required a sack to hold them all. It seems quite remarkable that Martin having been summons to appear in court could then make this claim that he had not brought along any paperwork whatsoever that might have added to his defence. It would appear that Howitt also provided no paper evidence so any judgement would have to be made based purely on verbal statements of the accuser and accused.

Evidence concerning the conduct of the tour was then given by pedestrian John Brighton and trainer Richard Lewis. Their statements confirmed what had been widely suspected in as much as the various races were arranged for maximum crowd excitement with the athletes running to Martin's instructions to speed up or slow down which he would orchestrate by moving the book he was apparently holding to record the laps and Deerfoot was scripted to take the eventual victory on every occasion. Strangely, the central character Deerfoot, was not required to appear at the court.

53/54) The WANDSWORTH COUNTY COURT in Garratt Lane was built in 1859-60 and the exterior has changed little during its long life. (Top picture c2010, bottom c1890). Since 1973 it has not been used as a Court House and subsequently has served a variety of community uses. In 1996 it became the Wandsworth Museum, while currently it is the Wandsworth Library. The carved royal arms are situated above the original public entrance which has now been partially blocked up to form a window.

55) THE COURT ROOM. An early view of the interior of the court house where George Martin was sued by William Jackson *'The American Deer'* for non payment of wages during the British tour.

A Mr Haynes, acting as Howitt's solicitor, said that his client's agreement to finish in a lower finishing position in the races should not have affected his receipt of the weekly wage that had been agreed between him and Martin.

Judge Fraser told Jackson he would take time to deliberate his decision. He regretted that a man of Jackson's fame should be involved in such matters while admitting that he took an interest in pedestrianism but that his position prevented him actually attending events and finally he said that he understood Jackson had been threatened by Martin and that as well as providing an officer to accompany him to the train station, he would jail for a month anyone who molested him.

Two weeks later on Thursday November 6 at the Garratt Lane courthouse again, Judge Fraser announced his decision. He found that Martin still owed Howitt a week's wages of £4 following the race held at Peterborough but the £2 claimed for two races in Ireland was not owed by Martin as the weekly wage agreement had been rescinded by then and Howitt was running on a pay by race agreement which had been honoured by Martin.

The case caused enormous reaction in the sporting press especially the revelations by John Brighton that the results had all been fixed in advance. The word fraud was used by many but George Martin remained unbowed by the adverse publicity surrounding him. He claimed the public had not been duped and that his 'circus' had merely been exhibitions of running and were not disguised as real races. Apart from this, the times achieved by Deerfoot demonstrated that he was a superior athlete.

Just four days after the court case, Deerfoot proved his outstanding running ability in a 1 hour race at the Brompton track. Passing 6 miles in 31:03 and 10 miles in 52:22 he was well on course for a new distance record for the hour and in the remaining 7 minutes 38 seconds he galloped on to set a new world record of 11 miles 720 yards (18379m) beating the previous best performance by 330 yards while John Brighton in second place set a British record of 11 miles 370 yards just 20 yards further than the distance achieved by Battersea's John Levett back in 1854.

Originally, John Garratt had planned a big 10 miles handicap to come off on Monday November 24 and thirteen entries from some of the very best men including Deerfoot, William Lang, Jack White, Teddy Mills, John Brighton and Harry Andrews had already been received but for whatever reason this idea was cancelled and became just a single 6 miles race featuring another appearance of the man of the moment, Deerfoot.

This would be his second competitive appearance at the Wandsworth track and was taking place just a month after the court case. The 6 miles match stake was for a £50 a side and would be against Alfred Day of Brighouse in Yorkshire. The race was remarkable for an amazing incident which resulted in quite extraordinary scenes. Day had beaten Deerfoot in a 1 mile race the previous year so was considered a worthy opponent although it was considered by some that the 6 miles distance might prove beyond his ability. Despite publicity efforts by John Garratt, including the promise of a strong body of policeman to deter pickpockets, at the appointed start time of 3.00 pm. the crowd numbered less than a thousand. They both went off at a fair pace with Deerfoot leading through the first mile in 4:52 and Day through the second passed in 10:10. After the half way point with Deerfoot leading in 15:33, Day began to fade and before the 4 miles mark was reached, he staggered off the track defeated.

The crowd were unhappy that the contest was now finished as Deerfoot was left to cover the final 2 miles on his own. As he went through the process he was joined by a spectator Mr R Purkes of Wimbledon who ran alongside him. This greatly annoyed the Red Indian who ran into the crowd, grabbed a stick from one of the spectators and waving it above his head proceeded to chase Purkes threatening to kill him. Luckily for Purkes and Deerfoot, others prevented any injury by intervening and taking the stick away from Deerfoot who then returned to the circuit to complete the final laps.

It was reported that the famed Deerfoot was back at the Garratt Lane track with a group of friends on Monday December 1 to witness a 7 miles walk handicap won by Turnham Green's William Spooner and a 1 mile handicap race for residents of Fulham and Hammersmith. 'The Gateshead Clipper' Jack White was also using the track for his training base as he prepared for his match against Teddy Mills due to come off at Hackney Wick on December 15.

By the end of 1862 in John Garratt's first complete year of ownership, over 75 different events had been held at the track not including the weekly shooting matches. If the Garratt Lane track had appeared to be in decline, Garratt's take over had certainly revived its fortune and it was now firmly back on the sporting map.

The opening match of 1863 was on the fifth day of the year and was an attractive 2 miles walk between the unbeaten short distance man from Blackfriars William Hatley and the long distance man Brixton's James Miles. Despite the poor weather with a bleak wind and pouring rain which was coming down in torrents and which had made the course very heavy, over 1000 spectators were attracted to the Copenhagen Grounds. An hour prior to the start the betting was 6 to

56) The prominent walker WILLIAM HATLEY (1840-?) was trained by John Smith 'The Regent Street Pet' and gained some success as a walker over the shorter distances.

4 on Hatley but had closed at 2 to 1 on him as just after 3.30 pm the men set off at a cracking pace with Miles immediately taking the lead but with Hatley sticking close to him as they passed the first quarter of a mile lap in 94 seconds. A circuit later Hatley had wrested the lead and he went through the half mile in 3:25.0. From that point onwards he increased his lead and at the half distance done in 7:22.0 he led Miles by 30 yards. Two laps later this lead had been doubled and by the conclusion of the 2 miles Hatley had won easily by some 70 yards in 15:38.0. The general opinion was that Miles was better suited to longer distances and was still requiring rest from his many arduous long distance races of 1862.

As well as competing, James Miles would often be at the Copenhagen Grounds to watch events, to train, or to assist

other athletes. For a 4 miles walking handicap match between two amateurs Mr Stuart and Mr Horton on February 21, Miles acted as assistant to Horton while Stuart was assisted by William Richards better known as 'The Welshman' and a future outstanding pedestrian himself. Assisting a pedestrian usually meant providing a drink or sponge when required and assistants quite often followed their men around the course for a lot of the journey.

Three days later, John Brighton 'The Norwich Milkboy', who had been one of George Martin's troupe on the Deerfoot tour and whose evidence had been so crucial at the trial, ran unsuccessfully in an 880 yards scratch race at the grounds against Tucker of Fakenham and was

57) JOHN BRIGHTON 'The Norwich Milkboy' (1831-1896) was holder of the 4 and 6 miles champions belts and also the 10 miles champions cup as well as setting a British one hour record of 11 miles 370 yards when finishing second to Deerfoot in October 1862.

58) JACK WHITE 'The Gateshead Clipper' (1838-1910) was one of the most successful British pedestrians of the nineteenth century at all distances from 1 to 10 miles. His 6 miles time of 29:50 was not beaten by a British runner until 1936. In his later life he was the trainer for Chelsea FC following their foundation in 1905. Although he never appears to have raced at Garratt Lane he was there many times as a spectator or as a helper for another pedestrian.

attended on by Jack White the famed 'Gateshead Clipper'. Brighton's previous outings at Garratt Lane had been back in 1855 on the old three laps to the mile circuit, when entering under a false name had caused his disqualification. In addition, he had been there to run unsuccessfully in the 6 miles handicap on John Garratt's Opening Day meeting of February 25 1862.

On Tuesday March 10, the day of the wedding of the Prince of Wales, the future King Edward V11 to Princess Alexandra, James Miles was back at the ground, not only competing but also to support his 10 year old brother John who was matched with another 10 year old John Harris and an 11 year old James Mills to walk a mile. Despite his family pedigree, young Miles failed by 6 yards to defeat young Mills. This unusual event was followed by James who was backed to walk seven and three quarter miles, 31 laps of the track, before Charles Sutton, who advertised himself as 'The Tooting Stag', could run the 40 laps necessary to cover 10 miles. With James achieving his walking task in 63:00, he defeated the man from Tooting, who required a further eighteen seconds to run his distance.

The following Tuesday, George Martin was chosen as referee and timekeeper in a match where 'Jack the fishman', whose real name was Jack Willings but was generally known as 'Spratty', had been backed by Mr Hinchcliffe of 'The Pencutters Arms', James Street, New Cut, Lambeth against Fred Chandler who supported 'Time', for £5 a side, to walk 5 miles within an hour while carrying a basket on his head containing a 56lb weight without stopping. 'Spratty' easily accomplished the task in 44:43 and no doubt used up some of his winnings in 'The Wellington Inn' before returning to London. In the same month, John Garratt's application for a full licence for the Inn was again refused by the local justices of the peace just as Bob Sadler's applications had been on so many occasions.

On Easter Monday April 6, James Miles defended the 10 miles handicap belt with £25 a side, against Brown of Kensington allowing him a two minute start. The challenge proved an easy one for Miles as 1:24.30 later, with a margin of just 6 yards but with plenty in reserve, he came home a very comfortable winner. On Whit Monday May 25, James expected a sterner test from Chelsea's Joseph Oliver in another challenge for the belt and £25 a side and he allowed his opponent a one and a half minutes start. Miles did his preparatory work at Redhill while Oliver used the Garratt Lane track for his training. Approaching the appointed start time of 5.00 pm and as the crowds of spectators parted with their sixpences (5p's) at the gate, John Garratt was chosen as match referee. In his 90 seconds start allowance, Oliver covered some 400 yards and was therefore almost a lap ahead of Miles as James set off in pursuit. The gap between the two men was a mere 2 or 3 yards as the four and a half miles point was reached. Two laps later and the halfway point, saw James hit the front and the match appeared all over, Oliver however persisted in a plucky

way but by the eighth mile with Miles getting further and further ahead, decided that he had no chance and pulled up leaving Miles to finish the distance unopposed to win the £50 and retain the champion belt.

On January 12 at Hackney, Deerfoot had improved his own 1 hour world record to 11 miles 790 yards (18425m) and at Brompton on February 23 he further improved this to 11 miles 880 yards (18507m). His third and final improvement of 1863 came on April 3, again at Brompton, when he ran a distance of 11 miles 970 yards (18589m) which was to last as a world record for the next 34 years, three world record performances in less than 3 months! What ever aspersions had been cast on Deerfoot's running ability in the Wandsworth Court case, to any doubters he had now proved beyond all argument that he was a very top class athlete.

An era ended when on May 16 Deerfoot boarded Brunel's ship 'The Great Eastern' to return to America. The man had ignited Pedestrianism in England and provided a memorable spectacle throughout the length and breath of Britain for the many thousands who had flocked to see him. His two racing appearances at the Garratt Lane track and the case held at The Court House as a result of his tour give him a prominent place in the sporting history of Wandsworth.

James Miles, the champion walker, played the part of a backer when he supported a man called Davis against Jack the Fishman on July 6 for a 5 miles walk with both men carrying a 28 lb weight but with Davis being allowed a 2 minutes start. Despite the lead Davis achieved during his allowance, Jack soon began to cut him back and after two and a half miles went to the front. A couple of laps later, facing a hopeless task, Davis resigned and although Jack Willings carried on for a while, James Miles approached him and told him that he did not require him to finish the distance as he considered his man Davis had been fairly beaten.

59) THE GREAT EASTERN Isambard Kingdom Brunel's ship, on which Deerfoot returned to America in 1863.

CHAPTER 15
1863-1864
A new owner George Woodey and 'The Crowcatcher' in Wandsworth

It appears that John Garratt's health had deteriorated during the first half of 1863 and that he had made the decision that he could no longer manage the facility and had decided to sell up.

On July 5 'Bell's Life' contained the following announcement:-

TO THE SPORTING WORLD To be SOLD, in consequence of the continued illness of Mr Garratt, the present proprietor, the lease, about 42 years, with possession, of the Copenhagen Running Grounds, Garratt Lane, Wandsworth. It is impossible by mere advertisement to state the eligibility of this property. It is in extent nearly five acres. 29,000 persons paid for entrance last year, largest sum taken on one day £70. It has a beautiful stream of water running through the premises supplied by an artesian well. The house and grounds are in excellent repair and when the South Western Railway make their station this house ought to get a licence. It has a wine licence. A party with £250 can purchase and should make a fortune. Apply for order to Mr Patching, 32 Cranbourne Street, Leicester Square'.

The reference to a new railway station would have referred to the one which was to be constructed at Earlsfield and originally called 'Earlsfield and Summerstown' but this would not actually reach fruition for another twenty one years in 1884, long after the track had passed into history.

John Garratt's lease on the ground was sold to George Woodey who was known as a trainer in various sports including pedestrianism and the prize ring. Certainly a George Woodey had acted as one of Jem Mace's seconds when he won the English heavyweight title in beating Sam Hurst at Southend on June 18 1861. Woodey made even more improvements to the facility, widening the running path and building of a 98 yards swimming

60) WILLIAM LANG 'The Crowcatcher' (1839-1905) was born in Stockton on Tees. At various times he won the Champions Cup at 1, 4, 5 and 10 miles and set a 1 hour record of 11 miles 871 yards. In 1863 the numerous trophies he had won were on view for a time at the Garratt Lane track.

pool presumably in the water channel immediately behind Althorp Lodge. By the end of the year it was called *'The Garratt Lane running, training and shooting grounds'*.

During the late Summer, *'The wizard of pedestrianism'*, George Martin, was having his mail directed to Garratt Lane and had possibly taken up residence in the cottage next to the track or *'The Wellington Inn'* itself and one of his protégées, William Lang *'The Crowcatcher'*, from Middlesborough was also there. At the end of August, *'Bell's Life'* advertised that many of Lang's trophies could be viewed at *'The Wellington Inn'* and that it was no mean collection, containing cups for the 12 miles, 10 miles and 4 miles, as well as the 5 miles belt. Lang certainly liked using the track for his training and during a quite remarkable year for him, he had set British records for 1 mile, 2 miles and 1 hour. In addition he had agreed to accept a wager to run 1 mile in the quite unheard of time of 4:15.0 with the backer of 'Time' laying down £50 to Lang's £25.

The event came off on Friday October 30 at Newmarket, in the presence of a large attendance. At about 9.30 am Lang came to the scratch line on the Cambridge turnpike and the run would be towards the town, finishing opposite the Betting Rooms. Lang was described as running with long lurching strides and while the first half mile was over very level ground, the last half was definitely downhill. Quarter mile times were given as 55 seconds, 1:54.0 and 2:56.0 and although much distressed at the finish, Lang's final 440 yards stretch of 66 seconds won him the bet by a huge margin recording the incredibly fast time of four minutes two seconds! Understandably, many doubted the veracity of this performance and George Martin announced that he was prepared to bet anyone £50 that Lang could run 1 mile on a turnpike road of

Martin's choosing, within 40 miles of London in 4 minutes! A remarkable claim, as a sub four minute mile would not be achieved on a proper running track for another ninety one years. It seems equally remarkable that no one appears to ever have taken up Martin's challenge.

On Tuesday November 3, the Garratt Lane track was used for some donkey races and an animal by the name of Billy and owned by Mr Spicer won the Final following some qualifying heats. Six days later this event resulted in a match being made for Mr Spicer's donkey to run against William Lang over 4 miles with 'The Crowcatcher' receiving a 440 yards start and the match to come off at Garratt Lane on Monday December 14. Lang seems only to have competed at the Wandsworth ground on one occasion previously, when he had won a 440 yards hurdles event in January 1862 but he had acted as a referee or timekeeper there on more than one occasion during 1863. He had forfeited a match there against James Pudney in February 1860 and unfortunately the proposed match with Spicer's donkey went the same way and never took place.

The Monday prior to the intended race, Lang had run 4 miles for the Champion's Belt against Sanderson of Manchester at the Bow running track. Over 1000 spectators expected to see a closely contested race as the men had run closely in a 5 miles contest at Hackney the previous week with Lang winning narrowly in front of some 3000 spectators. It seemed strange that prior to the event the odds showed Sanderson as the favourite at 2 and 3 to 1 and it was rumoured that something was up with Lang and so it proved, as after covering only the first mile he dropped out. The Bow crowd were very disappointed and apparently one of them struck Lang. He claimed that his failure to finish was caused by an injured foot but the general feeling was that he should not have begun the contest if he had not felt up to it and the punters had been swindled out of their money. 'Bell's Life' called the race a 'contemptible exhibition' and warned 'The Crowcatcher' that he should be careful about maintaining his good name. This foot injury having caused such consternation in East London became disappointment in South London as Lang forfeited the planned Garratt Lane race to Spicer and his donkey.

By the end of the year, both William Lang and his mentor George Martin had moved up to Manchester, George taking over the pedestrian ground attached to 'The Royal Oak' and Lang becoming the proprietor of 'The Navigation Inn'. Within a couple of years Lang would run the fastest 1 mile on record with a 4:17 ¼ performance at George Martin's track.

George Woodey's first year in charge virtually ended with a Grand Boxing Day Sports when he and Jesse Smith of 'The Proud Peacock' in Maiden Lane put up prizes for three handicap events a 150 yards, a 880 yards and a 3 miles walk. They received a huge entry by Garratt Lane standards and the 150 yards and 880 yards both required 6 heats while the walk attracted 40 entries. Delightfully good weather attracted nearly 2000 spectators down to Garratt Lane, some no doubt helped by the offer of commodious vans to transport them from 'The Proud Peacock' at a small fare for the double journey. The walk was decided on the day along with some other minor events and the finalists for the 150 yards and 880 yards were required to return on Saturday January 2 to contest the finals.

The improvements made to the grounds by George Woodey following on from those of John Garratt had certainly raised the standard of the facility which were now being advertised in 'Bell's Life' as:-

'The Garratt Lane Running, Training and Shooting Grounds. For training in all athletic exercises they are unequalled, with shower baths and other accommodation, and the champions in Peds and Pugs hail from here. The courses are the finest in England. Pigeon, sparrow shooting &c at all times on application, or privately with the best of birds in any quantity'.

Shooting such birds for sport might not be appealing today but in Victorian times when they were commonly sold as food, it seemed quite normal.

By April of 1864 'The Illustrated Sporting News' reported:-

'The Garratt Lane grounds can with justice now be pronounced second to none in the kingdom .... The running ground has been considerably improved, the path widened and the various courses were the height of perfection to try the speed of the competitors. Apart from the interest of the events decided, these grounds alone are worth a visit; with its fountain, the finest artesian well near London, fish pond and the fine piece of water............Here is a course of pure water 98 yards in length, on which our most noted professors of swimming, can decide their trials and thus stimulate all classes to learn an art which is alike important to everyone, individually or in a national point of view'.

This description of an idyllic setting worth a visit just to see its beauty is all a very far cry from the modern Garratt Lane where a virtually continuous line of traffic thunders by on a daily basis.

George Woodey obviously intended that his swimming channel should be used for competition and it was clear that he also intended to bring on as many young runners and walkers as well by confining his events to novice racing instead of the 'big name' pedestrians. This was evidenced by very large attendances of spectators and athletes at the Easter events of that year. In a 100 yards handicap race for novices, he offered a money prize for the winner but a pair of pedestrian shoes, for running or walking to the second and third placers. A sack race attracted 18 entries which required 6 heats and a Final, an especially reserved box for the visiting press was provided and to ensure good order, Sergeant Collins of V Division was there with other officers.

For many years the amateur sport of pedestrianism had thrived alongside the professional one. The universities of Oxford and Cambridge in particular were prominent and after holding their own college sports for some years, they had held the first ever Oxford v Cambridge athletics meeting at Christchurch, Oxford in the March of 1864. Amateur contests had been held at Garratt Lane previously and although termed 'amateur' there had been money wagers between the contestants. In the early days, the term 'amateur' had merely meant that the athletes did not pursue the sport as their main source of income, it did not mean that money would not exchange hands either in wagers or side bets. This much stricter code of amateurism was not to come into being until the formation of the Amateur Athletic Association which was still sixteen years away from fruition.

An amateur pedestrian event that attracted a large attendance and heavy betting to the Copenhagen Grounds was a 50 miles walk arranged for Saturday April 23. The prize on offer was a large silver cup and £40 gathered with a £10 contribution from each of the four contestants namely Frederic Stuart, W Horton, C Beaufort and A Bridge. Stuart and Horton had competed against each other at Garratt Lane previously when in February 1863, Stuart, looked after by William Richards the Welshman, had beaten Horton attended by James Miles, in a 4 miles walk, so it was quite common for professionals to assist amateurs. Strangely, Stuart was using a pseudonym as his real name was Frederic Pace having been born as such in Islington in 1841.

With Captain Cordington having been appointed as the referee, the event was to start at 9.00 am and after five hours, a gun would be fired to indicate a half hour's break for dinner when the men's distance achieved up to that point, would be accurately marked. The weather conditions were clear and warm and on setting about their 200 lap journey the men all appeared to be walking fairly and at considerable speed. At 10 miles Horton led in 1:36.48 and was been looked after by the well known cricketer Sheppard, while only 2 seconds behind him came Stuart, whose assistant was the professional walker William Myers of Newmarket. At 20 miles Stuart led in 3:20.50 but was only 15 seconds ahead of Horton who led Bridge by a further 5 seconds. Just prior to this point, Beaufort had retired so the contest was

now reduced to three. At 2.00 pm the gun was fired and Stuart was found to have covered 28¾ miles with Horton 570 yards behind him. Bridge had pulled up at 25 miles so as the gun went he was nearly 4 miles behind the leader but during the dinner break he indicated that he intended continuing the struggle hoping that one of the other competitors might break down.

Stuart got back on the track at 2:36 pm and had already covered three more laps before Horton began and who was now 1 mile and 130 yards behind him. Bridges, having renewed the contest reached a total of 31 ½ miles before finally giving up the contest. Stuart maintained his lead and at the finish was three quarters of a mile ahead of Horton. As he passed the referee at the finish, it was 6:58.05 pm so he had walked for 9 hours 58 minutes 5 seconds and allowing the 36 minutes he had used up at dinner time, he had accomplished the 50 miles in 9:22.05. Not surprisingly Stuart and Horton were very distressed at the end of their efforts but Stuart had the satisfaction of taking home the silver cup and the £40 winnings.

As well as the frequent races held at the grounds, George Woodey still promoted regular pigeon shooting events. On Monday May 2 thirty one competitors took part in a Derby Pigeon Handicap which Woodey had arranged in conjunction with Mr W Page. The conditions were that each competitor fired double barrelled guns with one ounce shot, at birds which were released from five traps and which traps were released for each competitor was decided by the throw of a dice. Mr Webb and Mr Nash having killed all their birds decided to divide the first and second prizes of £10 and £2.10.0 (£2.50) between them.

During his reign at the track the prizes offered by George Woodey began to take the place of the side bets. For his Whit Monday meeting on May 21 he had provided three silver watches and additional money prizes for three events, a 120 yards handicap which required 5 heats and a Final. A 3 miles walk handicap which had attracted 33 entries and sack races which needed 6 heats. The sack races caused an enormous amount of fun and excitement. The timekeepers were so convulsed in laughter during one heat that they failed to time the event at all. Mr Arthur became the eventual sack race winner as he slithered, jumped and hopped his way to a winning performance of 11.5 seconds. George Woodey was heard to say to him. *'I shall have to either bar you or put you a few seconds back, when next you come this way'*. Various other events finished off the competitions including that of a 14 year old boy who walked 1 mile in his ordinary clothes, including heavy boots, in 9 minutes 25 seconds and Mr Woodey and his family were congratulated on a very successful day which had entertained and amused so many.

'The Illustrated Sporting News' gave George Woodey and his grounds a glowing report, calling the event a 'triumph' and 'a perfect success in its fulfilment'. They particularly praised him in providing races for novices to encourage them and in bringing new blood into the sport. Their comment on condition of the grounds stated:-

'The grounds of themselves are really worth a visit, apart from any events to be witnessed, for there are fountains, flowers, water and other appliances to which few other locales can lay claim'.

Despite these glowing reports and all the various improvements, the grounds were apparently closed following an event there on July 25 1864 with a Sale Notice appearing in The Times the following day. The reason given in the press was that objections had been raised by local residents who obviously did not like the rowdy, gambling and perhaps heavy drinking crowds that were associated with pedestrianism.

'Bell's Life' on August 20 carried the following announcement:-

'Mr G Woodey, proprietor of Garratt Lane Running Grounds, wishes to thank his friends and those who supported him, and in connection with that late famed establishment he will ever remember the kindness and courtesy manifested to himself and family'.

Very strangely, a few events were still arranged at the track and reported on in the sporting press. On Saturday October 8 there was a 150 yards race when a man named Oliver beat another called Neckinger. 'The Illustrated Sporting News' reported on another 150 yards race between Collins and James on Tuesday October 11 which 'Bell's Life' recorded it as having taken place on Wednesday October 12. Either way, this appears to have been the final event ever to have taken place at the track and it did not end without dispute as the supporters of James wanted it declared as 'no race' when they claimed the starting pistol had not gone off properly. Their appeal was not upheld and whether correctly fired or not, the starting pistol had been fired for the last time at Bob Sadler's remarkably successful innovation.

'The Illustrated Sporting News' on February 29 1868 claimed that the ground had shut down due to the intolerance of some puritanical neighbours and also that the site now appeared to be a pasture ground.

In 1868 a man who was to become very prominent in the sport of athletics and in particular cross country running, Walter Rye, commented:-

'We soon shall have never a training place left, The Old Cope has vanished and Garratt Lane built on......how the deuce can a Londoner hope to get fit?'

Walter lived at various addresses in Wandsworth and presumably might have been present at some events at the Garratt Lane track and would, judging by his remarks, also have used it for training. He was quite a useful athlete himself and during his wholly amateur career was to win over 100 prizes for walking, running and cycling. At one time he employed the Garratt Lane favourite James Miles of Brixton to help him with his walking training and in his book 'An autobiography of an ancient athlete and antiquary' he mentions that he had seen Deerfoot run on October 14 1861 which was the day Deerfoot had raced against William Jackson 'The American Deer' over 4 miles at the Brompton track when Walter would only have been 18 years old.

In 1867, as a member of the 'Thames Rowing Club' who were based at 'The Red Lion' Putney, Rye instigated a cross country race to help maintain the fitness of its members and this led in 1868 to the formation of the first ever cross country club 'Thames Hare & Hounds' who based themselves at 'The Kings Head' in Roehampton. Because of this enterprise, Walter subsequently became known as 'the father of paper chasing' as that was the name given to the sport of cross country in its early days. He was a staunch supporter of amateur athletics and scathing about some of the practices prevalent in pedestrianism. To help create a new clean sport he was present in Oxford at the foundation of the Amateur Athletic Association in 1880. He was a noted antiquary and a prolific author particularly with books and papers on the history of the county of Norfolk where he had his family roots.. Following retirement, he moved from London to that county and in 1908 he was elected as Mayor of Norwich.

Following the closure of the track at Garratt Lane, the site was soon covered over and the ordnance survey map of 1865 shows 'The More Close Bleach and Dye Works' managed by Captain Elton and four cottages for workers, known as Elton's cottages as having been built on the southern side of the site as well as a large house which fronted on to Garratt Green at the eastern side. During the last twenty years of the nineteenth century, Franche Court Road and Huntspill Street had been laid out on the northern and southern extremities of the grounds and on the eastern side there were now three large houses facing Garratt Green. The tea gardens, ornamental fountains and orchards passed into history and Althorp Lodge itself disappeared at the

61) WALTER RYE (1843-1929) who bemoaned the loss of the Garratt Lane track.

62) A sale notice for the Althorp Lodge Estate appeared in 'The Times' on July 26 1864 and following the closure of the running track, the area where the track had been was quickly built on with housing and the Bleach & Dye Works. Although Althorp Lodge itself was not demolished until 1900, the ordnance survey maps during the next few years show how the lands surrounding the estate were redeveloped. Franche Court Road, Huntspill, Bellew and Squarry Streets were constructed and following the demolition of the Lodge, Burmester Road and Aldren Street appeared so that by the early years of the twentieth century all traces of the once famous Copenhagen Grounds had gone and became nothing more than a memory.

CERTAIN Freehold Premises, situate in Garrett-lane, Wandsworth, Surrey, formerly known as Althorp-lodge, but now called the Duke of Wellington Inn, having extensive frontage to the high road leading from Wandsworth to Tooting, and opposite St. Mary's Church, with garden, pleasure grounds, and meadow land, the whole containing 3½ acres or thereabouts, and possessing an artesian well, subject to a lease thereof for 43 years from 25th December, 1861, at £140 per annum. Also Freehold Ground-rents, amounting to £16 6s. per annum, secured upon five dwelling-houses (one with shop), being Nos. 8, 9, 10, 11, and 12, Edward's-terrace, Garrett-lane aforesaid ; and also a Freehold piece of Land, situate in Garrett-lane aforesaid, and adjoining the premises before-mentioned, having a frontage to the said high road of 152 feet 6 inches, and a depth of 656 feet 9 inches, adapted for building purposes. Particulars whereof and conditions of sale may be had gratis of Mr. T. H. Merriman, solicitor, 1, Mitre-court, Temple, London ; Mr. Wm. Venn, solicitor, 3, New-inn, Strand ; Mr. Henry Harris, solicitor, No. 34 A, Moorgate-street ; Mr. David Aston, solicitor, of 108, Edgware-road, W. ; Mr. R. Gibbs, solicitor, 18, Poultry, Cheapside, E.C. ; and of the auctioneers, 43, Chancery-lane, W.C.—J. A. Buckley, Chief Clerk.

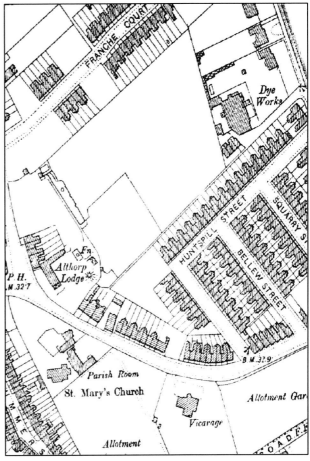

63) Ordnance Survey Map c1868

64) Ordnance Survey Map c1894

turn of the century having stood in Garratt Lane for over 100 years and in the same year, 1900, Burmester and Aldren road were constructed.

A group of shops fronting on to Garratt Lane then replaced Althorp Lodge and butted on to the existing Edwards Terrace. These were originally called Althorp Terrace but all of this group suffered extensively from bomb damage in the Second World War when an air attack in September 1940 took out both corners of Burmester Road and demolished or partly demolished everything from 749 to 773 Garratt Lane. The site then lay vacant for many years until the construction of Burmester House.

In 1900 the Anglo American laundry was constructed on the northern side backing on to the rear gardens of houses in Franche Court Road and in 1906 they purchased and then demolished eight houses in Burmester Road to construct a fine new laundry building that is still there today. Also by 1906, the Dye Works had become a laundry and it was later to become an Electrical Components Works. Burmester Road now leads into a pleasant low level housing estate constructed by Laing Homes in 1993 and as you walk up Burmester Road from Garratt Lane it is hard to imagine that you are retracing the steps of the excited if perhaps rowdy crowds that would flock into the grounds from Bob Sadler's *'Wellington Inn'* to

65) BURMESTER HOUSE in Garratt Lane on the corner of Burmester Road. This block of flats stands almost exactly on the site of Althorp Lodge.

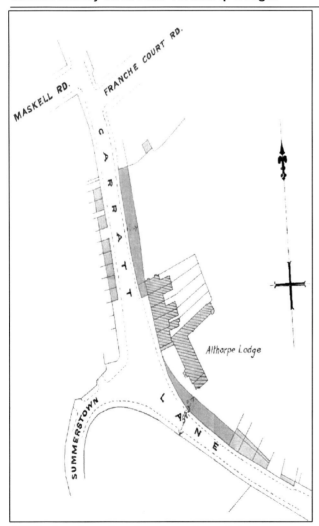

66) A drawing showing how Garratt Lane was to be widened in 1900 just prior to the demolition of Althorp Lodge. The five houses forming Edwards Terrace attached to the northern end of the Lodge, remained until badly damaged during world war two

witness races between some of the finest athletes of the nineteenth century.

In the early nineteen nineties two archaeological digs by the Museum of London took place on the site of the track prior to the construction of the housing estate by Laing Homes. The first one in July 1992 was on the original location of the Anglo American Laundry behind where the current building now stands in Burmester Road. The second dig in May 1994, was on the site of The More Close Bleach and Dye Works and the Laundry and Electrical components factory that had all followed the demise of the track.

Both excavations took place without the knowledge that for an eleven year period one hundred and forty years earlier, this site had been a major sporting venue. This lack of knowledge was clearly due to the fact that in the research carried out prior to the excavations, no ordnance survey maps that had been consulted had ever shown the existence of the running track. The fame that the track had enjoyed, the crowds it had attracted and the sporting stars that had trodden its cinders had all been forgotten with the passing of time. It is most unlikely of course that even if they had been armed with this knowledge that there would have been any archaeological finds relating to the track anyway.

During the excavations, which were really aimed at finding evidence of a much earlier site usage, there was the discovery of cinder which could have been the track surface, top soil which could have been from the ornamental gardens, foundations which could have been from changing rooms or a viewing stand for spectators. However, none of these were considered as a possibility as the archaeologists were blissfully unaware that despite its fame, the sports facility had ever existed there!

CHAPTER 16
The deaths of George Martin, John Garratt and Bob Sadler

If any man could have laid claim to have ignited and influenced the popularity of the pedestrian sport in England it was George Martin and no history of pedestrianism in Victorian times could possibly fail to mention his enormous contribution. Like many Victorians, he had packed an immense amount into his fairly brief life but the promoting wizard's final days were very sad and his end came rather suddenly at the early age of 39.

Following Deerfoot's return to America in 1863, George moved his family back up to Manchester and on November 28 announced that he had taken over *'The Royal Oak'* in Newton Heath. This was one and a half miles from Manchester on the main road to Oldham just 600 yards from Miles Platting railway station and George spent a lot of money upgrading the athletic grounds attached to the public house. The facility opened on April 16 1864 and included a rabbit coursing course forming a circle of 750 yards, an American trotting and galloping track, a bowling green and wrestling arena, shooting grounds and a huge 650 yards running track 9 yards wide plus a 460 yards straight track also 9 yards wide. Not surprisingly, this huge sports ground occupied some 20 acres. He also advertised a shower bath 'the best in existence', for the use of the public for a charge of one penny which included a towel and soap and not least, a portable dressing room for competitors *'to strip by the fireside right against the starting post'*.

In the summer of 1865 just as the facility began to really take off, George started to show a sign of mental illness the same affliction his father had suffered similarly with tragic consequences only eleven years earlier and on September 22 the ground was advertised for sale. George was confined in a private lunatic asylum Wye House in Buxton where he was diagnosed with acute mania. However, after only a week's incarceration he was discharged. Subsequently he somehow made his way to London and was eventually found wandering in Trafalgar Square. From there he was taken to *'St Martin's Workhouse Infirmary'* near Charing Cross where he died on Saturday October 21 1865 aged only 39. A small obituary in the press stated:-

'......he died of a rupture of a blood vessel on the brain caused by his struggles to release himself whilst secured to his bed'.

The following Thursday he was buried in a common grave at Finchley cemetery which remains unmarked to this day. Apart from his family, only Bill Price, the renowned trainer and proprietor of the famous track at Hackney Wick, attended the funeral. Despite the large sums of money that had passed through his hands,

67) The grave of GEORGE MARTIN (1826-1865) in the Finchley cemetery, Unmarked grave D821.

George Martin had left his wife and six children destitute as his creditors reclaimed most of his £2000 estate but fortunately for Alice and the children, the eldest of whom was only thirteen, his friends gathered round to raise some funds on their behalf.

After John Garratt left *'The Copenhagen Grounds'* in Wandsworth due to ill health, he subsequently became the publican at *'The Denmark'* public house on Old Brompton Road where he lived with his wife Hannah, son Alfred and daughter Alice and that is where he died on November 21 1871 aged 52. At the time of his death, his son was only 9 and his daughter 5. Like George Martin before him and despite his enormous success as a pedestrian promoter he had not become a rich man. His final resting place was a common grave in Brompton Cemetery and also like Martin's, the grave is unmarked.

Despite the fact that he was no was longer responsible for the athletics track, Bob Sadler and his family stayed in the vicinity of Summerstown and Bob

68) Now a restaurant but formerly *The Denmark*' public House in Old Brompton where John Garratt died in 1871.

69) The unmarked grave of JOHN GARRATT (1819-1871) in Brompton cemetery. Common grave 65872 compartment X west wall.

continued to ply his trade as a beer seller operating from *'The Wellington Inn'*. It would appear he left the premises about the time that the grounds closed and Althorp Lodge was now being lived in by Thomas Griffiths and no longer operating as a beer house. In October 1864 Bob was granted a licence to use a cow house and the directory of 1869 shows him living back in Summerstown and managing *'The Corner Pin'* which was next door but one to the cottage he had been living in with his parents and new wife back in 1841. By 1871, Bob was living in number 12 of the group of twelve cottages at the Plough Lane end of Church Street (Summerstown) known as 'Sadler's Cottages' with his wife Jane and daughter Martha. This would have been the last cottage on the eastern side of the road next to where *'The Hare and Hounds'* formerly *'The White Lion'* public house stands but which itself closed in 2011. There seems to be no evidence that these cottages, despite their name, had any connection with Bob or his family but they well might have done so as Bob's ancestors had a long association with Wandsworth.

His son John had married Sarah Eastland at St Leonard's Church Streatham in 1865 and the same year he took over the running of *'The Prince of Wales'*, Garratt Lane from David Palmer. John and Sarah had three sons Robert James born in 1866, John in 1868, William George in 1870 and a daughter

Annie in 1874. By 1881 they had moved from *'The Prince of Wales'* back into 22 Church Street, *'The Sir Jeffrey Dunstan'*, where he had lived as a boy with his parents. Whilst living here previously, John would have seen the construction of the original *'Prince of Wales'* in 1852 and would now witness that building's demolition and subsequent rebuilding in 1898.

The 1881 census shows Bob, Jane and Martha living at Burntwood Cottage which stood on the corner of Burntwood Lane and Garratt Lane and a few years later they moved into a newly built double fronted property built in 1884 by Dunstan and Smith of Garratt Park, Tooting called Copplestone House which is now 811 Garratt Lane and still bears this name on its front wall. Bob lived the remainder of his life there until he died in the premises on Sunday August 16 1896 in his eighty third year. He was buried the following Friday at the Wandsworth Cemetery in Magdalen Road, where on his very fine gravestone there is an inscription bearing the sentence:-

'Here lies one who was beloved by all and despised by none'.

At the time of his death he was quite a wealthy man. He left four cottages, numbers 16 18 20 and 22 Summerstown, to his wife Jane, which on her death were to go to his son John and then on to John's children. He left Copplestone House with its contents

70) Two of the houses left by Bob Sadler in his will. On the left is number 8 Copplestone Terrace and on the right Copplestone House which was built for him in 1885 and was where he died in 1896. These are now 809 and 811 Garratt Lane.

DEATH OF "BOB" SADLER.

At the advanced age of 85, Mr. Robert Sadler, familiarly known in sporting circles as "Bob Sadler," died on Sunday at his residence, Copplestone House, Garrett Lane, Lower Tooting. At a time, long since gone, when the manufacture of silk was carried on in the neighbourhood of the Wandle, Mr. Sadler was a bleacher of the article and a designer of its patterns. He subsequently became the owner of the celebrated training and running ground at Garrett Lane, where, as an old athlete and an amateur pugilist of no mean order, he trained many men who have since come to the front. He always maintained a high character for respectability, and was known for many acts of benevolence. The funeral took place at the cemetery, Wandsworth Common yesterday (Friday).

71) The obituary notice for Bob Sadler that appeared in the *South London Press* on August 22 1896.

and the house next to it, now 809 Garratt Lane, to his daughter Martha. A gold watch and chain to his eldest grandson Robert James and various sums of money to his son John, to his grand children and to his surviving siblings, brother William and sister Rachel.

Strangely, he never seemed to have lived in any of the four cottages in Summerstown which he left in his will. He would appear to have purchased these when they had come up for sale in September 1881 and had just used their rents as a source of income. In 1897, following his father's death, Bob's son John arranged for proper drainage to be installed at the rear of these cottages.

The six addresses Bob was in for the six census reports covering fifty years were all within a few hundred yards of each other, so he must have been a very well known personality in the Summerstown area.

1841 Summerstown, 1851 22 Church Street *'The Sir Jeffrey Dunstan'*, 1861 Althorp Lodge *'The Wellington Inn'*, Garrett Lane 1871 12 Sadlers Cottages, Church Street, 1881 Burntwood Cottage, Garrett Lane 1891 Copplestone House, Garrett Lane.

His wife Jane continued to live in Copplestone House with her daughter Martha until her own death aged 87 on March 25 1903 when she was buried beside her husband in Wandsworth Cemetery. On his retirement a couple of years later, John and his family moved from *'The Sir Jeffrey Dunstan'* then known as 47 Summerstown, since the renaming and renumbering of Church Street in 1887, into a newly built house at 2 Vicarage Terrace, now called 694 Garratt Lane, following the renumbering of Garratt Lane in 1906 and this house was situated almost exactly opposite his sister Martha in Copplestone House as it still is. *'The Sir Jeffrey Dunstan'* in Summerstown subsequently became a coffee shop and was later a second-hand shop prior to its demolition.

72) The fine polished granite headstone to ROBERT 'BOB' SADLER (c1813-1896), his wife JANE (1821-1903) and their daughter MARTHA (1844-1930) which is in the Wandsworth Cemetery, Magdalen Road. Block 5 grave 5055.

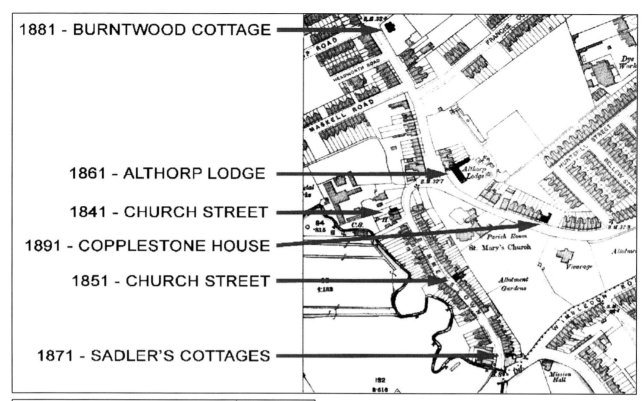

1881 - BURNTWOOD COTTAGE

1861 - ALTHORP LODGE

1841 - CHURCH STREET

1891 - COPPLESTONE HOUSE

1851 - CHURCH STREET

1871 - SADLER'S COTTAGES

74) Number 694 GARRATT LANE originally known as 2 Vicarage Terrace, where Bob Sadler's son John had moved after leaving 'The Sir Jeffrey Dunstan' in Summerstown.

73) The c1894 ordnance survey map showing where Bob Sadler was living for the six census returns between 1841 and 1891. At this time the area behind Althorp Lodge, where the running track had been, was now occupied by housing and the Dye Works.

The 1835 original St Mary's Church had been demolished and an Iron Church had been erected as a temporary structure before the new church in Wimbledon Road was constructed. Church Street had been renamed Summerstown and both sides are closely packed with houses.

The triangle of church Glebe Land still only contained the church, the school, the parish room and the vicarage but soon it was to be divided by Keble Street and packed with housing.

On the other side of Garratt Lane, Burmester and Aldren roads have still to be laid out on the land which once saw some of the top athletes in England perform and which attracted huge and very excited crowds to view their performances.

John died aged 80 in 1920 and was buried in Streatham Cemetery, Garratt Lane. His wife Sarah survived him by seven years until she joined him aged 89 in 1927. His sister Martha had moved from Copplestone House by 1922 and she was living at 5 Charlmont Road Tooting at the time of her death aged 86 on October 21 1930 and she was subsequently interred with her parents at the Wandsworth, Magdalen Road cemetery.

75) Garratt Lane in 2013 looking towards Wandsworth with Tesco Express, formerly *The Prince of Wales* public house, on the left at the entrance to Summerstown and Burmester House on the right at the corner of Burmester Road.

76) A 2013 view over the housing estate which now covers the site of the running track. The view is looking towards Garratt Lane with the rear of the 1906 Anglo American Laundry building in Burmester Road dominant in the distant right hand side. Behind the tree in the even more distant centre, is the back of Burmester House which stands on the site of Althorp Lodge alias Bob Sadler's *'Wellington Inn'*.

77) Tesco Express, formerly *'The Prince of Wales'* public house in Garratt Lane on the corner of Summerstown with the two cottages, one of which housed the Sadler family in the 1840's and *'The Corner Pin'* public house (1924) in the background.

78) The Sadler family in the Isle of Man during Christmas 2012. Back Row left to right:- Elizabeth, Robin and Charlotte. Front Row left to right:- Robert 'Bobby', Scarlette, Ruth and Summer.

John and Sarah had parented four children, Robert, John, William and Annie. Robert did not marry and Annie appears to have died at a young age. John was a seaman and married Phoebe Rose in the temporary iron church of St Mary's Summerstown before moving away to her family's roots in Cornwall. William married Alice and they initially lived at 90 Lavender Road, Battersea and later at 26 Keble Street before moving into 694 Garratt Lane in 1927 following the death of William's mother Sarah who had lived there with her son Robert. He died aged 78 in St James's Hospital Balham in January 1940 and was buried in his parent's grave at Streatham Cemetery, Garratt Lane. His brother William died aged 77 in St Francis's Hospital, Dulwich in October 1948 and William's wife Alice survived him until 1961 when she died aged 85 both she and William are buried in Streatham Cemetery although in a separate plot from Robert and his parents.

William and Alice had three children who were all given the traditional Sadler family names of Robert, William and John. The eldest child Robert married Ellen Carter and they had one child Betty Gwendoline. Robert died in a nursing home in Somerset in 1989 while Betty married David Phillips and they moved away to live in the Isle of Wight. The second son William married Florence Nicols and they lived in Swaby Road, Earlsfield and had eight children.

79) THE SADLER FAMILY TREE

WILLIAM SADLER m ELIZABETH	ROBERT ROOK SPINNEY m 1) ANNE HARMAN m 2) ELIZABETH RICHES

1 JAMES SADLER (1785-c1852) m **1 ANN SPINNEY (1779-c1852)**
2 Rachel Rook (1786-1846)
3 Sarah Harman (1789-?)
4 John Harman (1791-?)
5 Robert Rook (1801-?) m Sarah Larkins

1 Ann (1808-?)

2 Elizabeth (c1810-?)

3 James (c1812-1855)

4 ROBERT ROOK SADLER (c1813-1896) m JANE HUGHES (c1816-1903)

5 William (1826-?) m Mary Olfield (1831-?)

6 Rachel (1831-?) m Joseph Banister

1 Ellen (1838)

2 JOHN SADLER (1840-1920) m SARAH EASTLAND (1837-1927)

3 Martha (1844-1930)

1 Robert James (1866-1940)

2 John William (1868-1915) m Phoebe Rose (1868-?)

3 WILLIAM GEORGE SADLER (1871-1948) m ALICE HOLLOWAY (c1876-1961)

4 Annie (1874-?)

1 Robert John (1904-1989) m Ellen Carter

2 William George (1907-1974) m Florence Nichols

3 JOHN SADLER (1914-1993) m EVELINE SANDERS (1912-1997)

1 ROBIN MISCHA SADLER (1941) m MARGARET CLAGUE (1940)

1 Ruth (1967)

2 ROBERT SADLER (1968) m CHARLOTTE HARDING (1976)

1 SCARLETTE FELICITY SADLER (2004)
2 SUMMER AVA SADLER (2008)

The third child John married Eveline Sanders and they moved to Macclesfield during World War 2 and had one child Robin Mischa who now lives with his wife Margaret in the Isle of Man. They had two children, daughter Ruth and son Robert who also lives in the Isle of Man with his wife Charlotte and their two little children Scarlett and Summer who are of course the great, great, great, great (4) grand daughters of Robert 'Bob' Sadler.

Robert 'Bob' Sadler had seen immense changes during his long life in the Summerstown area. His childhood would have been spent playing in local fields and no doubt fishing in the river Wandle. He would have known the Surrey Iron Railway which passed directly through the area before its closure in 1846 and also the original 1852 'Prince of Wales' public house built directly over ground where the railway tracks had been. There would have been only a handful of cottages in the Dunsford, Garratt and Summerstown communities but towards the end of his life he would have seen an enormous amount of building activity as these small hamlets on Garratt Lane were joined up by more and more housing and as scattered groups of cottages and farms fell to urban development. The construction of 'Earlsfield and Summerstown' station in 1884 was a major cause of further building along Garratt Lane which was becoming a continuous line of houses offices and shops between Wandsworth and Tooting. He would surely have known all the local and visiting sporting personalities and it is unimaginable that he would not have shaken hands with or at the very least have spoken to, George Martin and the legendary Deerfoot.

Little remains of the Summerstown area that would have been familiar to Bob Sadler. Althorp Lodge which he had styled as 'The Wellington Inn' was demolished at the beginning of the twentieth century and now Burmester House, on the northern corner of Burmester Road, is virtually exactly on its site. The 1852 'Prince of Wales' public house was demolished and replaced in 1898 with the building which closed in March 2012 which Bob would never have seen and which this year (2013) has been adapted and become a Tesco Express. As previously stated, during the life of Althorp Lodge, five houses, one of them a shop, were built on a section of the ornamental gardens at the northern end of the building and were known as 'Edwards Terrace' and these were the last strong connection with the sporting facility to survive. Their demolition, following extensive bomb damage in 1940, saw the final demise of any buildings which had been contemporary with 'The Copenhagen Grounds' although there are small fragments of the first one still left attached to the end of number 747 Garratt Lane. This would have been number 8 Edwards Terrace and subsequently was number 749 Garratt Lane. Opposite Edwards Terrace on the other side of Garratt Lane, stood an even older terrace of seven shops including a post office and known as Church Row, these butted on to the northern side of the 'Prince of Wales' but all these houses and shops are now gone. Also gone is the first church of St Mary's and its Vicarage. The school which was situated between the Vicarage and the church and which Bob's children might well have attended, has also passed into history. A small block of flats occupies the site of the Vicarage itself but the old wall that defined

80) Above: It was fitting that for a time leading up to the London 2012 Olympic Games, there was a Visa advert on the side wall of 747 Garratt Lane which featured Usain Bolt the current 'fastest man on earth' shown running towards where Bob Sadler's track had been some 160 years earlier.

81) Right: A fragment of wall still attached to 747 Garratt Lane which would formerly have been part of number 749 and which prior to the renumbering of Garratt Lane had been 8 Edwards Terrace. The terrace was a group of five houses attached to the north side of Althorp Lodge alias 'The Wellington Inn' in the early 1860's.

one side of its grounds is still there next to number 700 Garratt Lane. Bob would have seen the construction of the St Clement Danes Almshouses by the corner of Wimbledon Road which were opened in 1849 and also the construction of the two large cemeteries, Lambeth Cemetery in Blackshaw Road covering forty one acres in 1854 and the thirty six acre Streatham Cemetery in Garratt Lane in 1892.

The only properties now left which have any strong Sadler family connections are the cottage at number 6 Summerstown where the family were living in 1841, Copplestone House at 811 Garratt Lane where Bob died in 1896 and the house next to it, 809 Garratt Lane, which Bob also owned. In addition, the house on the opposite side of the road, number 694 Garratt Lane, where later, his son John lived. There is also of course the very fine polished granite gravestone of Bob, his wife Jane and their daughter Martha at the Wandsworth Cemetery in Magdalen Road.

Robert 'Bob' Sadler had played a very prominent part in the life and sporting history of Wandsworth. It is sad that today he is not a name that is commemorated locally in some way and that the sporting personalities that visited Wandsworth because of his enterprise, are also not remembered in the small low level housing estate facing Garratt Green that now covers the scene of their athletic exploits. His idea of a sporting facility, which was further embellished by John Garratt and George Woodey during their tenure, had put Garratt Lane and Wandsworth on the Victorian sporting map. Huge crowds were attracted to the area which must have been of great benefit to local businesses at the time and it is quite extraordinary that the story of *'The Copenhagen Grounds, Garratt Lane, Wandsworth'* has remained forgotten and hidden for so long.

82) The unintentional series of amusing signs which greet those attending the regular Car Boot sales on the car park of Wimbledon Greyhound Stadium, which very appropriately lead towards *'The Corner Pin'* and beyond across Garratt Lane to where the Victorian pedestrians plied their sporting trade.

BIBLIOGRAPHY

Fifty years of my life
(Sir J D Astley) 1894

Industries of Wandsworth past and present
(Cecil T Davis) 1898

Memoirs of Robert Patrick Watson
(R P Watson) 1899

An autobiography of an ancient athlete and antiquary
(Walter Rye) 1916

The story of Wandsworth and Putney
(G W C Green BA c1924

Days that are gone
(Alfred J Hurley) 1947

Links with the past - Old inns, taverns & Coffee Houses of London
(Thurston & Co Ltd) 1966

The Annals of Thames Hare & Hounds
(James Ryan & Ian H Fraser) 1968

The Kings of Distance
(Peter Lovesey) 1968

The Mayor of Garratt
(Anthony Shaw) 1980

Retracing the first public railway
(Derek A Bayliss) 1981

Huguenots in Wandsworth
(R A Shaw, R D Gwynn & P Thomas) 1985

Inn and around London A history of Young's Pubs
(Helen Osborn) 1991

Picture the past The way we were Volume 3
(Anthony Shaw) 1995

The boroughs of Wandsworth & Battersea at war
(Patrick Loobey & Jon Mills) 1996

The first running grounds c1835-1870
(John Goulstone) 1999

Front Runners
(Warren Roe) 2002

Deerfoot athletics' noble savage
(Rob Hadgraft) 2007

Edward 'Teddy' Mills 'Young England' 1841-1894 Champion east-ender
(Warren Roe) 2010

Sporting lives
(Dave Day and Samantha-Jayne Oldfield) 2011